Do-It-Yourself

FLUTE

BY EMILY MORGAN-BOOTH

To access audio and video, visit:
www.halleonard.com/mylibrary

Enter Code
5206-8234-1270-4688

ISBN 978-1-70513-483-2

Visit Hal Leonard Online at **www.halleonard.com**

World headquarters, contact:
Hal Leonard
7777 West Bluemound Road
Milwaukee, WI 53213
Email: info@halleonard.com

In Europe, contact:
Hal Leonard Europe Limited
1 Red Place
London, W1K 6PL
Email: info@halleonardeurope.com

In Australia, contact:
Hal Leonard Australia Pty. Ltd.
4 Lentara Court
Cheltenham, Victoria, 3192 Australia
Email: info@halleonard.com.au

CONTENTS

SONG INDEX

INTRODUCTION

Playing the Flute

Welcome to an amazing community of flutists! You are joining thousands of others around the globe that call the flute their instrument of choice, including greats such as James Galway, Jeanne Baxtresser, Jean-Pierre Rampal, Bobbi Humphrey, Jasmine Choi, and Ian Anderson. The flute is an instrument that has been around for centuries and is one of the oldest instruments in existence. The modern flute looks and sounds a lot different than its beginnings. It is versatile, frequently found collaborating with other instruments, and easily transported anywhere. The characteristic sound of the flute lends itself to many genres of music, several of which are incorporated into this book. Let's get fluting!

This book has been created for aspiring flutists with little to no experience, carefully crafted to walk you through each step from the very beginning. This includes information about how to select a flute, assembly, playing position, reading music, and, how to play some of the most iconic songs and melodies spanning multiple genres and decades. As you peruse the book, it may be tempting to skip around to your favorites; however, it is important to follow the book in a linear fashion. Each song in the book builds and progresses from the previous song. Playing them in the order they appear will yield the most positive and satisfying results.

There are over 180 songs that reinforce topics covered throughout the book. Whether your favorite genre is rock, pop, classical, country, rap, R&B, musical and movie soundtracks, or traditional folk songs, you are sure to find some old gems and new favorites. Enjoy the journey, and welcome to the inner circle of the flute world!

Choosing a Quality Instrument

Finding a quality instrument that meets both your musical needs and budget can be tricky. Establishing how much you are willing to spend on an instrument is a good starting point. Once your budget is set, take time to utilize your resources and weigh your options. Talk with local musicians in your community; they can be a wealth of knowledge in narrowing your search. Stop at your local music store. Reach out to your friends on social media. Ultimately, you want to find an instrument of quality that is going to help you reach your goals.

About the Audio

On page 1, you will find a unique code. Go to **www.halleonard.com/mylibrary** and enter that code to gain access to audio and video online, for download or streaming. There you will find expert video instruction to get you started on the right foot, plus video and audio demonstration of many songs found in this book. These spots are indicted throughout the book by these symbols:

Also included is **PLAYBACK+**, a multi-functional audio player that allows you to slow down audio without changing pitch, set loop points, and pan left or right—available exclusively from Hal Leonard.

LESSON 1:
Assembly and Maintenance

Parts of the Flute

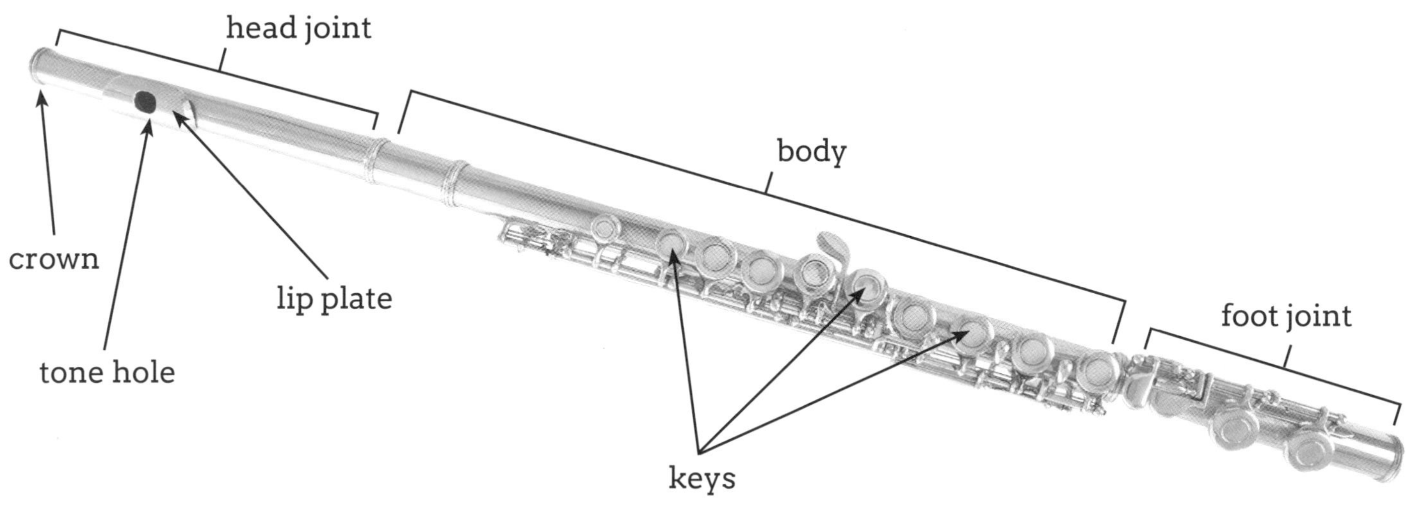

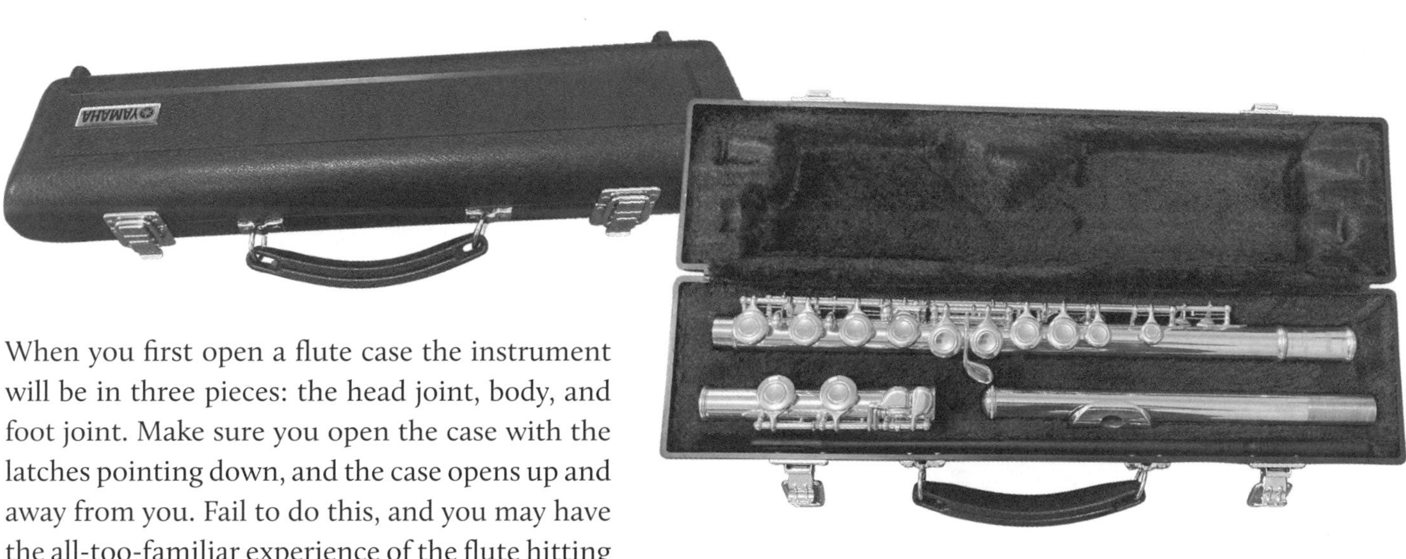

When you first open a flute case the instrument will be in three pieces: the head joint, body, and foot joint. Make sure you open the case with the latches pointing down, and the case opens up and away from you. Fail to do this, and you may have the all-too-familiar experience of the flute hitting the floor with a terrible crashing sound.

Assembly

Learning how to assemble your flute the correct way will save a lot of time and frustration later on.

1. Set your flute case down on a flat surface. Make sure the latches of the case are pointing down.
2. Undo the latches and open your case. Mindfully pick up the body and head joint. The body has a lot of moving parts; always pick it up by a large section instead of by a single key or rod. This is the part of the flute that can most easily break and need repairs if you are not careful.
3. Gently insert the head joint into the body. The first key on the body should be lined up with the tone hole of the head joint. Some flutes may have lines engraved on both joints to help with alignment.

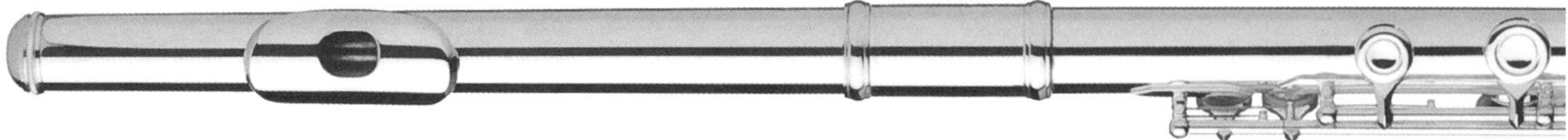

4. Once the body and head joints are properly aligned, carefully pick up the foot joint and insert it into the other end of the body. The rod on the foot joint should line up with the center of the last key on the body.

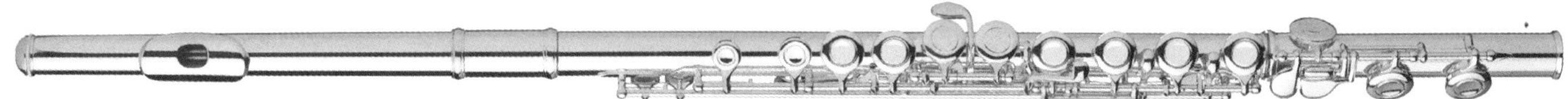

Care and Maintenance

Taking care of your flute is vital to keeping it in good playing condition. Take the time to clean it out after each practice session. Your flute will require less maintenance and extend the life of the instrument.

Cleaning Tools

- **Cleaning rod:** Usually comes with your flute; if not, you can pick one up at a local music store.
- **Cotton cloth:** A thin material that easily slides through the inside of your flute. You can purchase one, but you can also make one from an old cotton t-shirt. Toss it in with your laundry once a week for optimal cleanliness.
- **Silver polishing cloth:** This must be purchased but is inexpensive and lasts for years. Do not put this through the washing machine, as this will remove the polishing qualities of your cloth.

Daily Cleaning Routine

- Pick up the cleaning rod and cotton cloth. Thread the corner of the cloth through the eye of the cleaning rod. Gently push the cleaning rod through your flute beginning with the foot joint, continuing through the body, and ending with the head joint.
- Use the silver polishing cloth to clean the outside of your flute.
- Store the cotton cloth in a separate pouch or pocket than your flute and NOT directly on top of the flute.

LESSON 2:
Position and Tone Production

Hand Position

Left Hand Position

This is by far the trickiest part of holding your flute. Take time to study the picture and watch the video.

- Hold an imaginary cup with your left hand. Your thumb should go on the backside of the top half of the body. It should hover over/push down the longer "oar" key.
- Next, your pointer finger should hover over/push down the second key from the top of the body.
- Your middle finger should hover over/push down the fourth key from the top of the body.
- Your ring finger should hover over/push down the fifth key from the top of the body.
- Your pinkie finger should hover over/push down the sixth key from the top of the body. This key looks a lot different from the rest and sticks out a little.

Practice holding your flute with just the left hand to gain stability. Your flute should feel cradled by the space between your thumb and pointer finger.

Right Hand Position

- Find the bottom three keys of the body. These are the keys where your pointer, middle, and ring fingers should hover over/push down.
- Your thumb should rest beneath the pointer and middle fingers, adding crucial support.
- Your pinkie should hover over/push down the first key on your foot joint.

Practice holding your flute with both hands together. Consider putting small stickers (make sure they are easily removable) on the keys your fingers hover over/push down. This will help you remember your hand position with ease, especially when first starting out.

Points of Contact

For proper playing position, the points in which the flute makes contact with your body are your face, the crook of your left hand (between pointer finger and thumb), and your right thumb.

Posture and Breathing

Proper posture and breathing are essential for success as a flute player, and long-term health and wellness.

Posture

- Start by sitting in a chair. Sit tall with your feet flat on the floor. This should feel comfortable and stable. Make sure your back is straight. If you are sitting in a chair that hinders your ability to sit tall, choose another chair or scoot your bottom forward and sit towards the front half of the chair's seat.
- Standing is oftentimes a preferred way of achieving excellent posture for many flutists. However, this can be difficult at first, especially when learning to breathe properly, so use a chair to start.

Breathing

- Check your posture and make sure you are sitting properly.
- Place your hands on your waist and take a deep breath. Minimize any chest or shoulder movement, focusing your air downward, and feel your lungs expanding with air.
- After taking a deep breath, with your hands still on your waist, hold your air in for a few seconds. Notice your abdominal muscles contracting to hold in your air.
- Next, hiss the air out of your mouth. Try extending your breath to last for double digits. Ten seconds? Twenty? More?

Make sure you check out additional breathing exercises in the video, including techniques for a proper inhale/exhale, pushing a ball across the floor or countertop, and keeping a piece of paper against the wall.

Embouchure and Tone

Developing a proper embouchure will yield the best tone possible. Before playing your entire flute, it is crucial to spend time with the head joint ONLY.

- Pick up the **head joint** of the flute with the **crown** held by the thumb and index finger on your left hand with your right hand supporting the other end of the head joint.
- Bring the **tone hole** towards your lips. The larger part of the **lip plate** should rest underneath your bottom lip.
- Make a "poo" face with your lips. This will bring the lips to the correct shape, drawing the corners of your lips back slightly.
- Using the "poo" face, take a deep breath and push your air across the tone hole of the head joint. This is similar to creating a sound on a bottle, except a flutist aims their air downward a bit more.
- It is normal to have trouble with this at first, that is why starting with only the head joint is so important. Watch the video closely for additional help.
- Sometimes thinking about the image of "spitting rice" is helpful. The hole your lips make (called the aperture) needs to be quite small.
- Using a mirror while forming an embouchure and creating a tone is especially beneficial.

Head Joint Exercises

Try these exercises for the head joint to solidify your embouchure and tone production.

- **Long tone:** Play a tone on your head joint for as long as you are able. Try it with the end of the head joint covered. Then, try it with the end of the head joint uncovered.
- **Slide whistle:** Turn your head joint into a slide whistle! Using your right-hand index finger as the slide, move it in and out of the end of the head joint. You can even create simple songs like "Hot Cross Buns" and "Mary Had a Little Lamb."

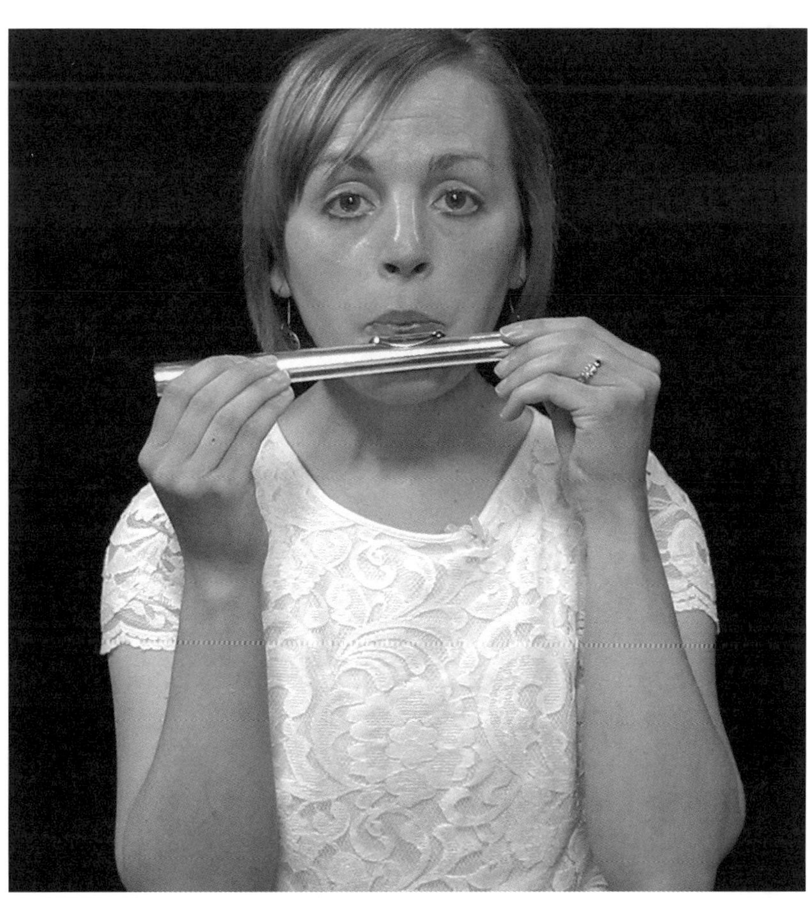

LESSON 3:
Understanding Music

This lesson is an overview of reading music. You are encouraged to reference these pages as you encounter the concepts throughout the book.

The better a person gets at learning the language of music, the more fun playing can be! Music is broken down into the basic elements of reading notes, rhythms, dynamics (how loud or soft the music should be) and articulations (how hard or soft to tongue the notes). We'll talk about notes and rhythms now and get into dynamics and articulations later in the book.

The Staff

Music is organized on a staff of five horizontal lines. It is capable of displaying virtually all there is to know about a piece of music. Two important things it shows us is how music moves over space and time (rhythm) and how high or low the notes are (pitch).

Rhythm is organized horizontally along the staff. Pitch is organized vertically using the lines and spaces; the higher a note's placement, the higher the pitch.

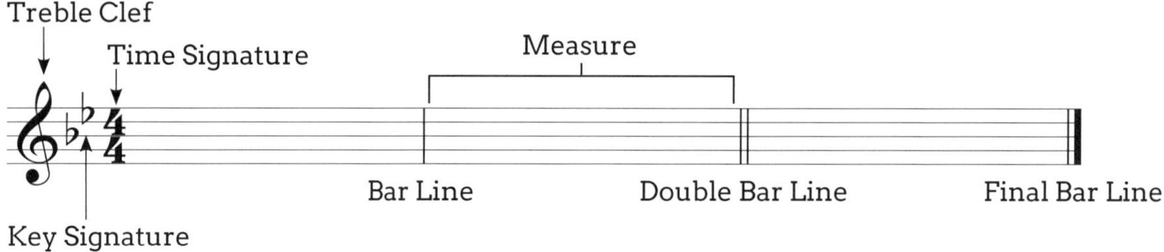

Treble Clef

The treble clef establishes the second line as the note G. The symbol itself is an ornate G, also known as a G Clef. Notice that it curls around the second line to establish G. There are other clefs, but the flute only reads in treble clef.

Bar Lines

Bar lines divide the staff into measures. A double bar line is used to mark something significant that occurs in the music, such as a new section. The final bar line is used to mark the end of the song.

Measures

A measure is the space between bar lines. It is also known as a "bar." The movement of music (rhythm) is established from left to right through this space.

Time Signature

The time signature determines how many beats are in each measure and what type of note receives one beat.

Key Signature

The key signature assigns either sharps or flats (never both together) for particular notes for the duration of the song. This is covered later in this lesson as well as in Lesson 5.

Spaces

Notes in the spaces in ascending order happen to spell the word FACE.

Lines

An acronym commonly used to remember notes on the lines in ascending order is Every Good Boy Does Fine.

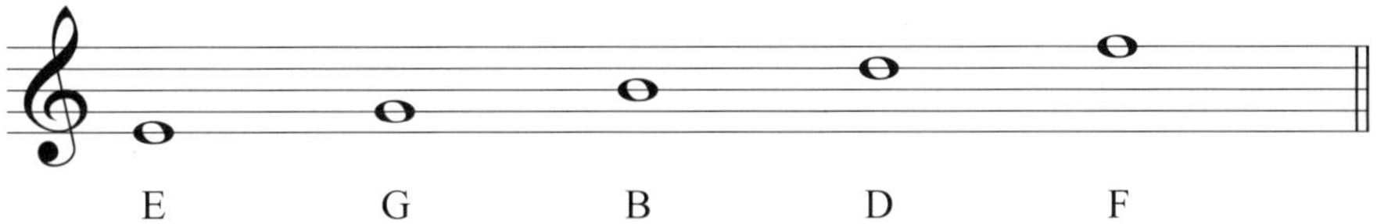

Alphabet

When the spaces and lines are combined, you will see that music ascends alphabetically from A to G. You may find it helpful to memorize and locate A as you learn.

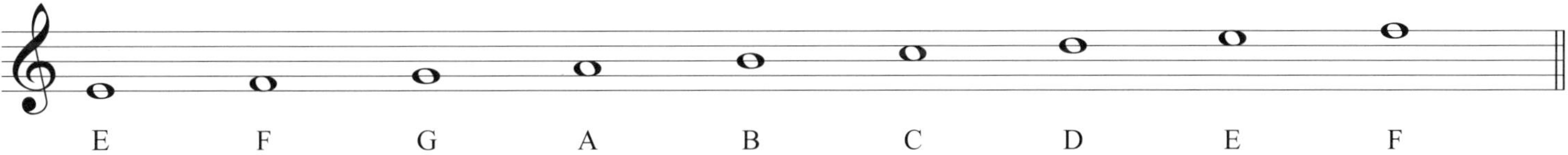

Ledger Lines

The staff can be thought of as an infinite number of lines; five of them are visible and the rest are invisible. When a note is needed above or below the staff, small lengths of line become visible. For instance, high B is in the space above the first ledger line. Low C is on the first ledger line below the staff.

Notice that this is a continuation of the alphabet.

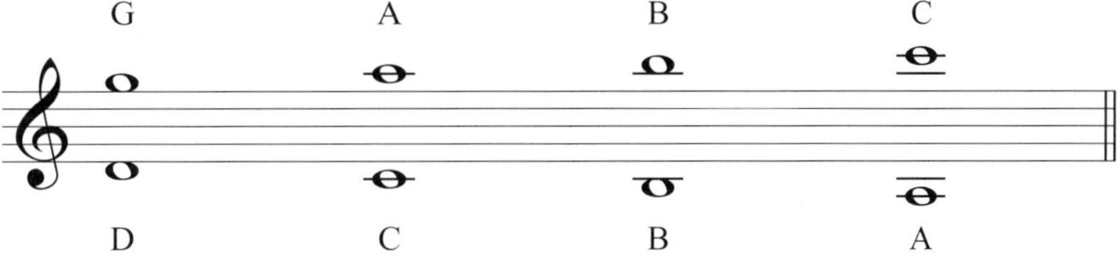

Accidentals

A half-step is the smallest interval (distance) between two notes. A note is altered by one half-step the following three ways:

An accidental applies to a note for one measure. In this example the last note does not require a natural to cancel the flat; this is accomplished by the key signature.

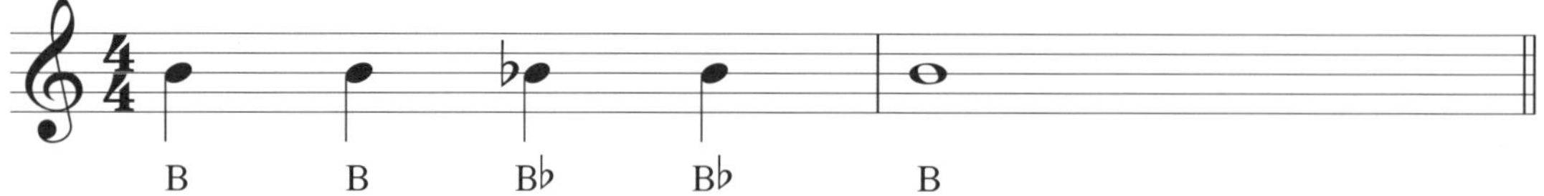

Sometimes you will see a courtesy reminder in parenthesis. This example will sound the same as the previous example.

Here are two examples of accidentals in the context of a key signature. This key signature assigns flats to all B's and E's. The natural symbol cancels each one until the next measure. Notice there is no courtesy reminder in the second measure.

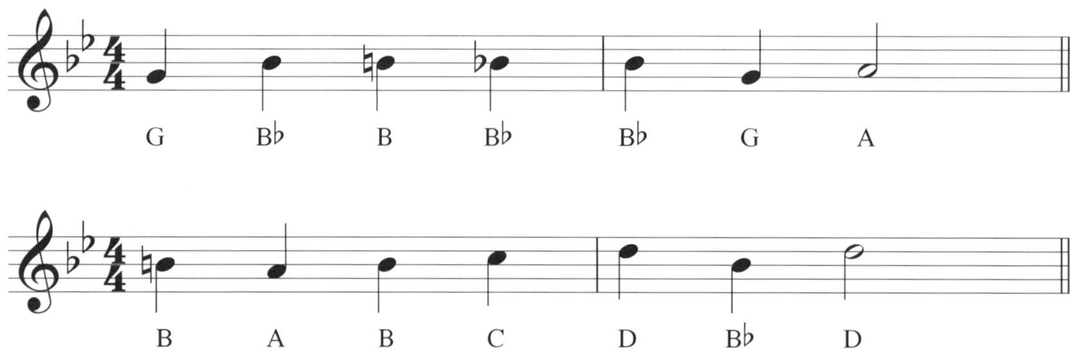

Rhythm

Time Signatures

Rhythm is based on evenly spaced pulses that we call beats. The distribution of beats is determined by the time signature. The top number represents how many beats are in each measure, while the bottom number represents what kind of note receives one beat.

There are 4 beats per measure
A quarter note ♩ is one beat

There are 6 beats per measure
An eighth note ♪ is one beat

Note and Rest Durations

The most common time signature is 4/4 time. The bottom number in 4/4 determines the following durations, whether sound (notes) or silence (rests):

WHOLE NOTE & REST
Each is four beats

HALF NOTE & REST
Each is two beats and one half of a whole note

QUARTER NOTE & REST
Each is one beat and one quarter of a whole note

EIGHTH NOTE & REST
Each is 1/2 beat and one eighth of a whole note

SIXTEENTH NOTE & REST
Each is 1/4 beat and one sixteenth of a whole note

Beams

Eighth notes and sixteenth notes are joined by horizontal beams, typically in groups of two and four. Eighth notes can be joined together with sixteenth notes, as you will see in Lesson 17.

Counting Method

In this book, we will count rhythm using the method shown in the chart below. Note durations from the previous page have been placed into a table with sixteen columns. This table is always theoretically present in a musician's thinking when playing in 4/4 time. It represents all the ways notes and beats can be divided into smaller parts.

Subdividing

Subdivide notes in order to keep your place and play with rhythmic accuracy. This is done by thinking internally, tapping a foot, or using a metronome. You can do this right now: whistle, hum, or simply exhale while tapping your foot and counting in your head (stop on 5). You just performed a whole note.

Another example of subdividing that you can do right now: clap four quarter notes while counting eighth notes: "1-&-2-&-3-&-4-&" (& = and). You will say a number on each clap with &'s between claps. We call the numbers downbeats, and the &'s upbeats.

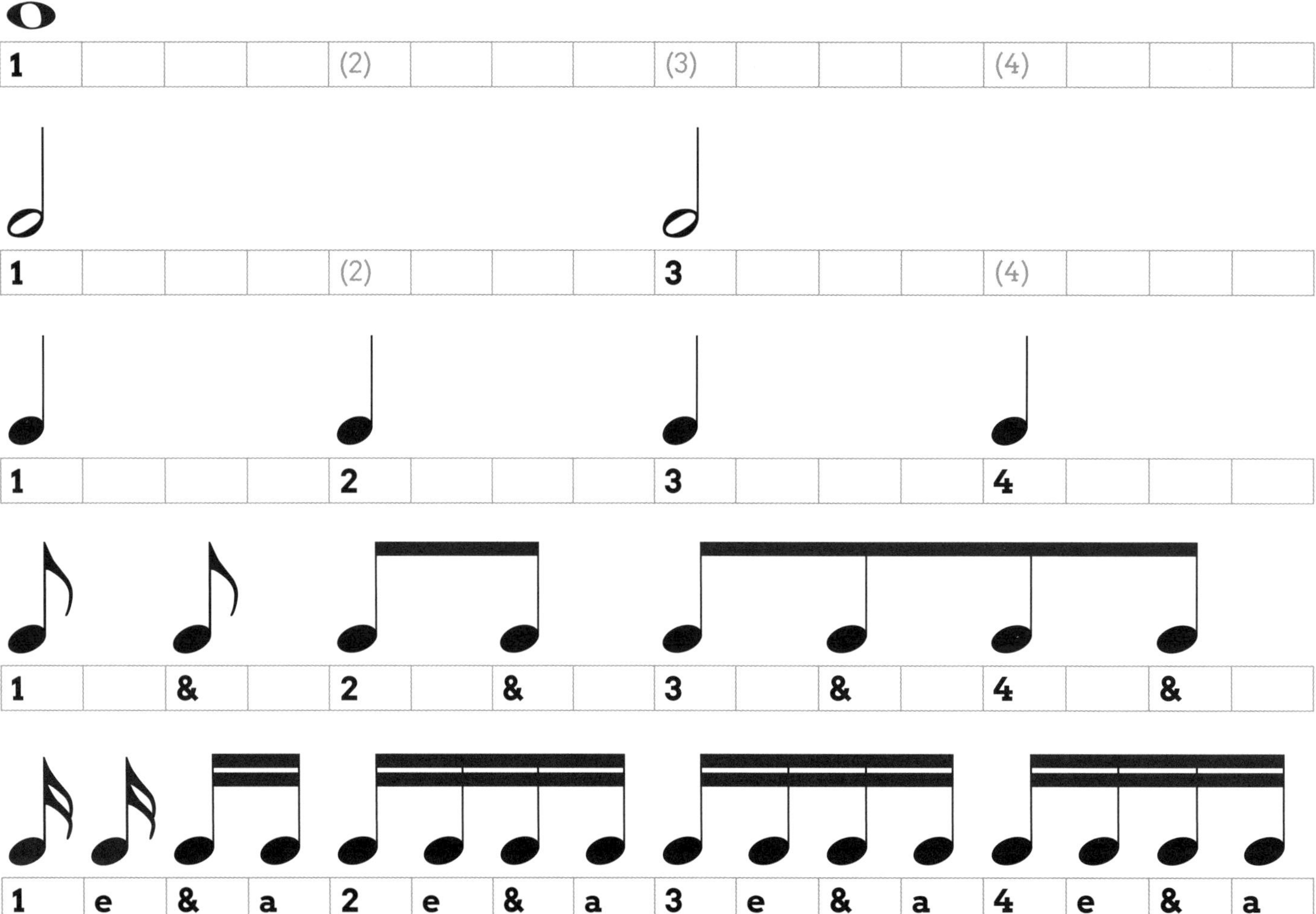

Rests

Rests are counted and subdivided just like notes but are silent. Some rests are added here with the counting italicized in parentheses.

Try counting the half note in the second line like this: while clapping the downbeats, say a long "one" and stop on the third clap.

Ties

A tie is an arc that joins two notes of the same pitch together. In this example two quarter notes are tied and become a single note worth two beats. Ties are not to be confused with slurs which use the same symbol, but connects notes of different pitches. Ties will be covered in Lesson 6.

Addition

As you saw with ties, rhythm involves a little math. Notice beat four of the sixteenth note line (bottom right of table). There is an eighth rest instead of two sixteenth rests because it is more efficient: 1/4 𝄿 + 1/4 𝄿 = 1/2 𝄾

Another bit of math we do involves dotted rhythms. This is covered in Lesson 6.

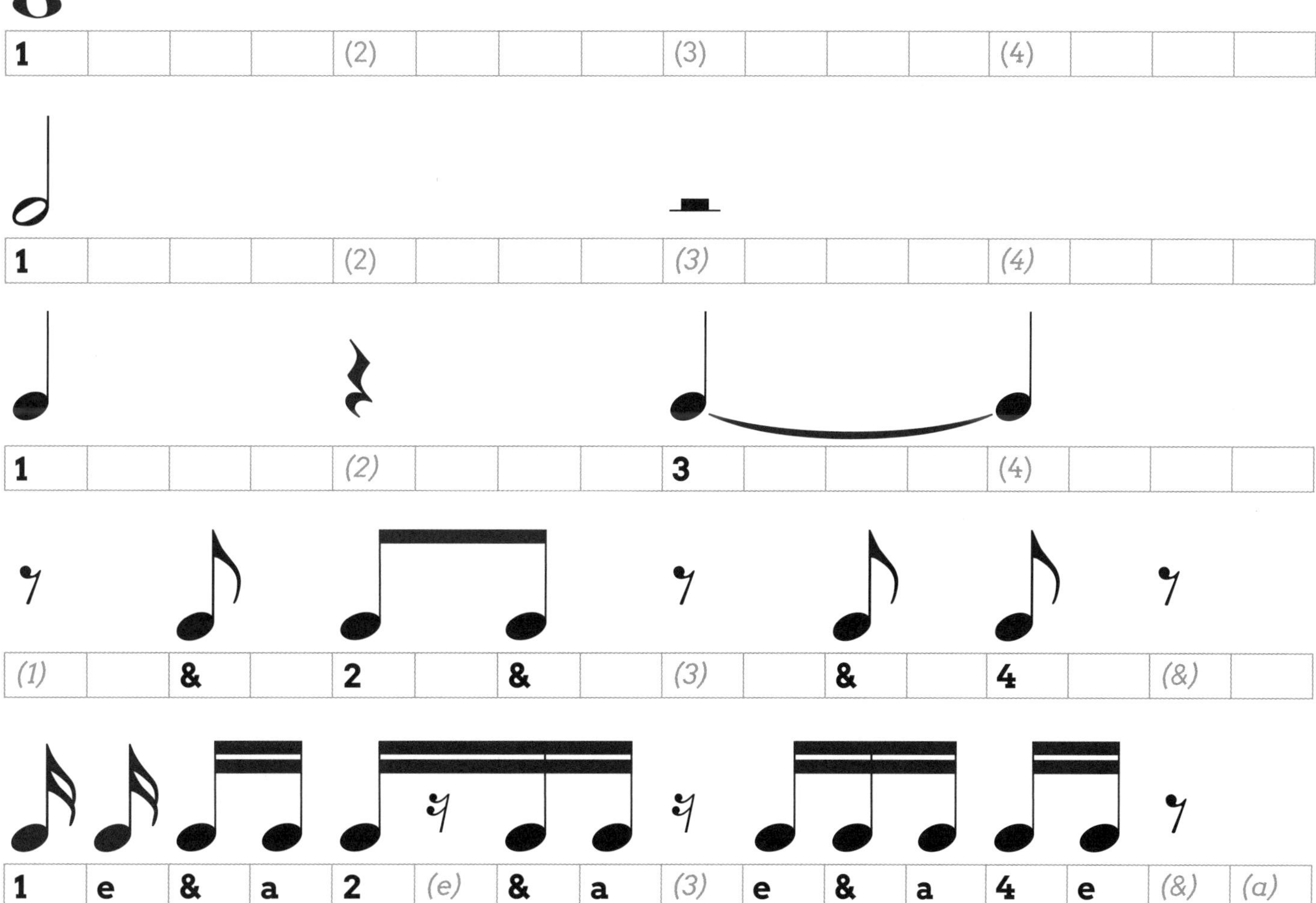

LESSON 4:
Reading Notes and Fingerings

As we introduce notes we will use a graphical system for showing fingerings. Below is the fingering for "D." The thumb key is located on the bottom left part of the graphic. The left half of the graphic is for the left hand. The right half of the graphic is for the right hand. The left and right hands are separated by a line. A *black circle* indicates the finger *is* pushing the key down. A *clear circle* indicates the finger *is not* pushing the key down.

D is played using the following fingering:

New Note: D

Whole Note

A **whole note** receives four counts (or beats) of sound in 4/4 time.

Whole Rest

A **whole rest** receives four counts (or beats) of silence in 4/4 time.

Drill: Rabbit Ears D

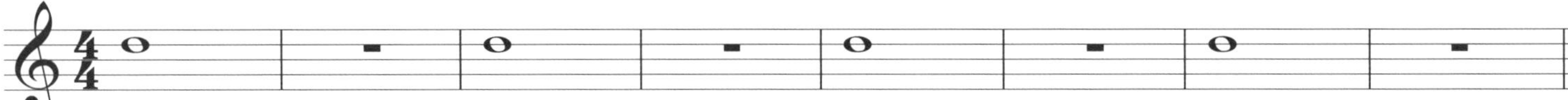

New Note: E-Flat

Drill: Add a Pinkie

FLUTE TALK

Tonguing

Now that you have played a couple of notes, it is time to start learning how to properly articulate these notes with your tongue. Always start each note by *tonguing*. This is done by moving your tongue as if you were saying "too." The tip of your tongue should touch the hard palate of your mouth, which is located behind your top teeth.

Drill: Back and Forth

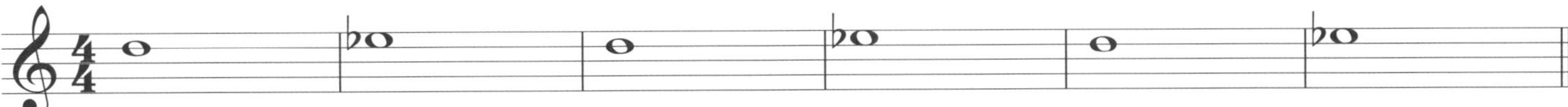

New Note: F

Drill: Learning "F"

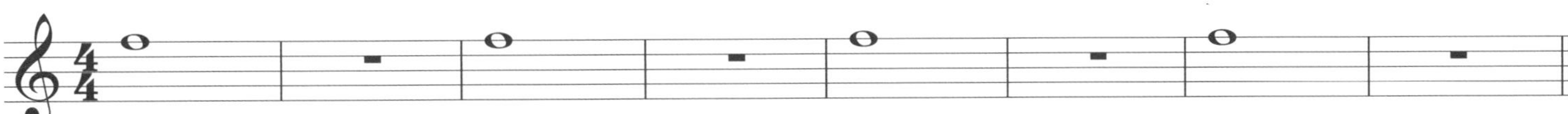

Half Note

A **half note** receives two counts (or beats) of sound in 4/4 time.

Half Rest

A **half rest** receives two counts (or beats) of silence in 4/4 time.

Drill: Half It Out

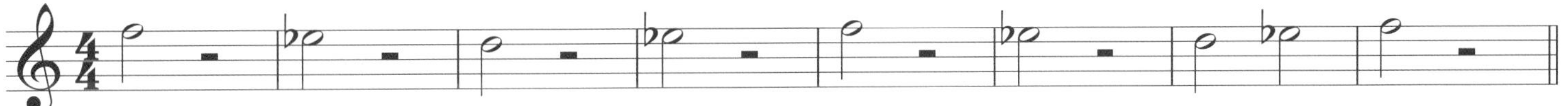

New Note: C

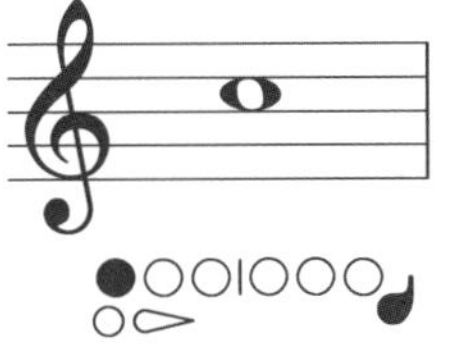

Drill: Nice to C You

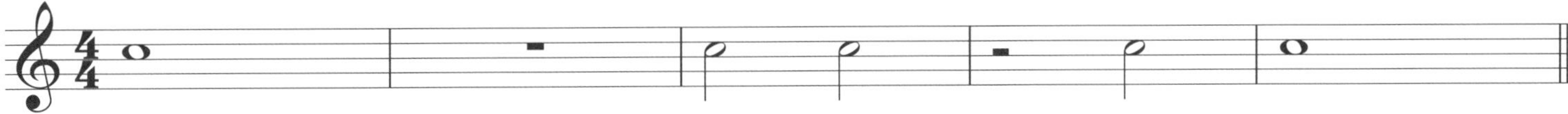

The C to D Transition and Down-Up Exercise

The C to D transition is a tough one! To go from C to D you must swap which fingers are down and up as you move between the notes. The *down-up exercise* is helpful to practice this transition. Rest the head joint of your flute on your left shoulder while keeping your fingers in position. Watch your finger movement and slowly practice moving back and forth between the fingerings for C and D. Make sure your fingers are moving together, gradually increasing the speed of your finger switches as you become more comfortable. You can use this technique on any tricky finger switches.

Drill: Tough Stuff

TOOLBOX

Looking Ahead

One technique many musicians use is referred to as *looking ahead.* During rests and long held notes, look ahead to anticipate your note and fingering changes. This mentally prepares you for what is to come in the music.

Drill: Fab Four

TOOLBOX

Accidentals—Good for an entire measure!

An *accidental* is a sharp, flat, or natural sign that appears in music. Accidentals are good for an entire measure. For example, in the next exercise you see flat symbols before the B's, making them B-flats. In measure three, the second note is also a B-flat, even though there is no flat symbol in front of it.

New Note: B-Flat

Drill: B-Flat

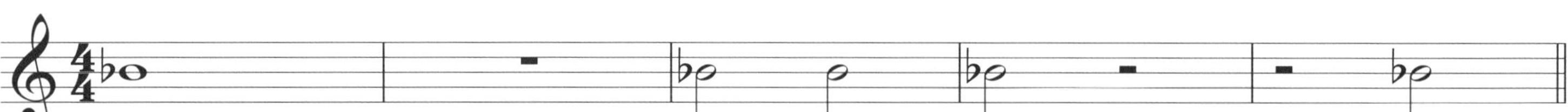

Drill: First Five

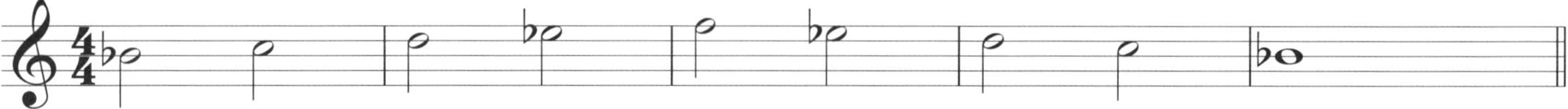

Quarter Note

A **quarter note** receives one count (or beat) of sound in 4/4 time.

Quarter Rest

A **quarter rest** receives one count (or beat) of silence in 4/4 time.

Drill: Faster First Five

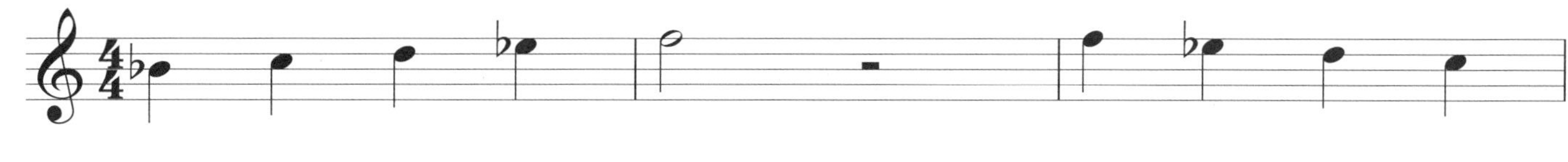

HOT CROSS BUNS

Traditional

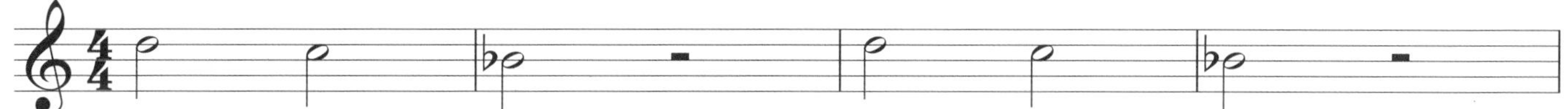

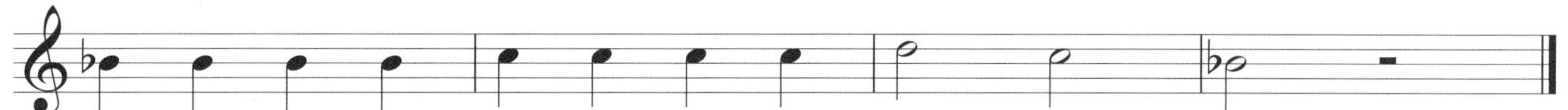

MERRILY WE ROLL ALONG

Traditional

WE WILL ROCK YOU

Words and Music by Brian May

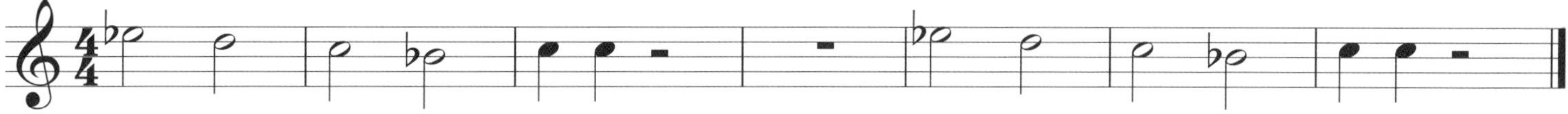

TOOLBOX

Breath Marks

A ❜ in the music indicates to take a breath. It is okay to end a note slightly early to take a breath. You will often see breath marks every two or four measures. If a song does not have any breath marks, breathe quickly when you need more air. Rests in your music are always free breath marks.

GO TELL AUNT RHODY

Traditional

LESSON 5:
Key of B-Flat

Key Signature

A *key signature* indicates whether to play a note sharp, flat, or natural. Flat ♭ or sharp ♯ signs are placed after the treble clef. The line or space that the sharp or flat occupies indicates which notes are changed.

Key of B-Flat

This key signature has two flats: B-flat and E-flat. Every time you see a B or E, you need to play them as B-flat or E-flat.

LIGHTLY ROW

Traditional

LOVE ME TENDER

Words and Music by Elvis Presley and Vera Matson

New Note: G

Drill: Learning G

FLUTE TALK

High Notes 

Although you will eventually be learning notes much higher than "G," it is important to understand how to develop an embouchure with the flexibility to play high notes. Here are some tips and tricks:

1. Use a higher angle of air.
2. Make your aperture smaller (think "ooo").
3. Use faster, colder air.

AU CLAIR DE LA LUNE

French Folksong

TOOLBOX

Pick-Up Notes

Pick-up notes are one or more notes that come before the first full measure. The beats of pick-up notes are often subtracted from the last measure. In the next exercise, notice that the first note is on beat four, and in the last measure, there are only three beats as the fourth beat was moved to the beginning. This justifies the single beat at the beginning.

In popular music, it is becoming increasingly common to not justify the final measure, as will be done in this book.

A-TISKET A-TASKET

Traditional

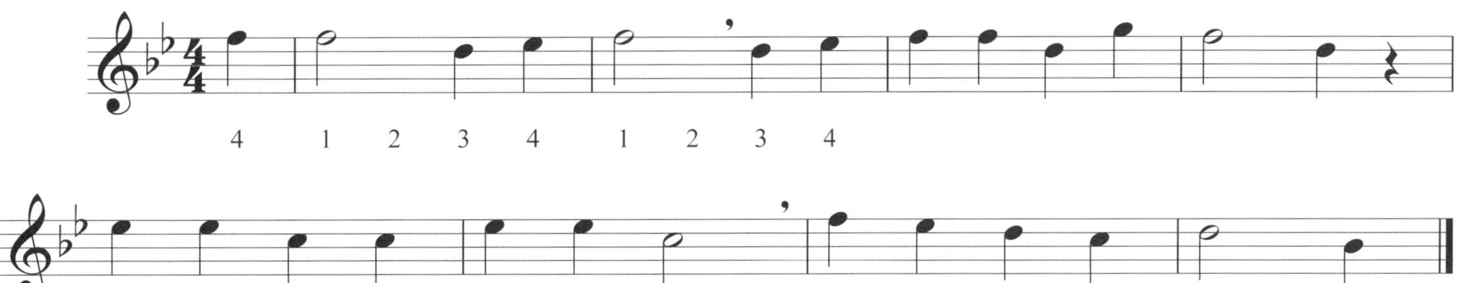

NOBODY KNOWS THE TROUBLE I'VE SEEN

African-American Spiritual

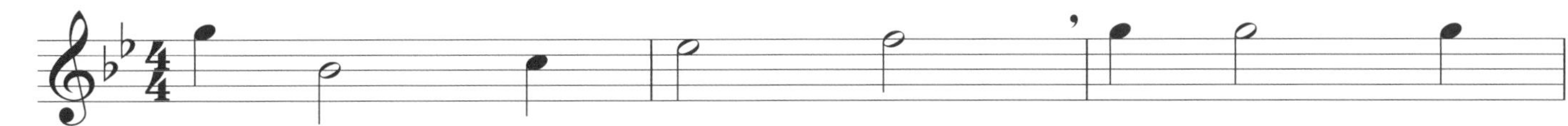

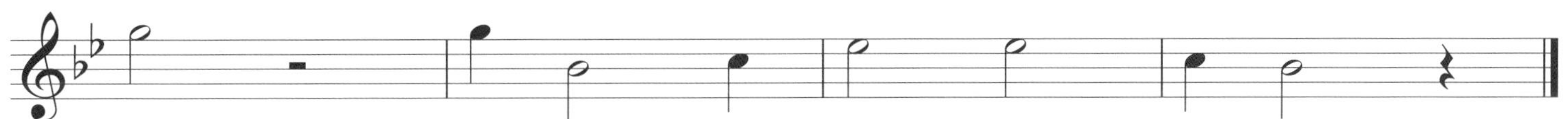

RAIN, RAIN GO AWAY

Traditional

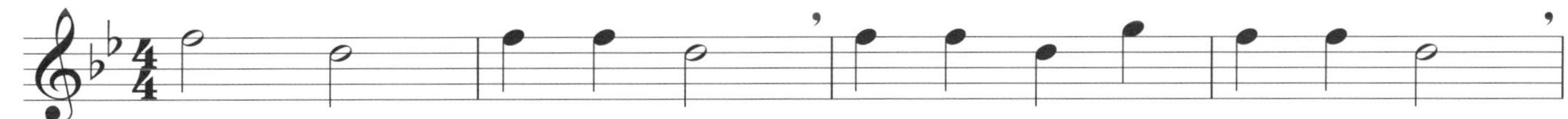

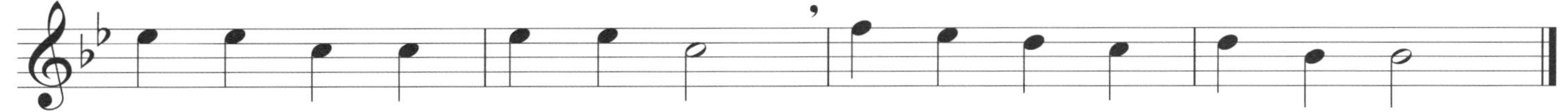

LONDON BRIDGE

Traditional

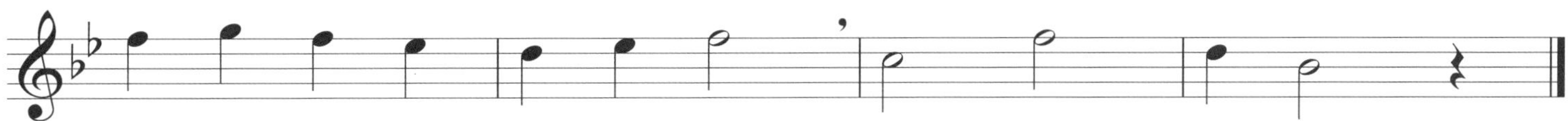

TWINKLE, TWINKLE LITTLE STAR

Traditional

TOOLBOX

No Breath Marks?!

Whenever no breath marks are indicated, breathe when needed. Once you are comfortable with the music, try to take a breath every two or four measures. To take it a step further, think of the melody as a singer, and take a breath when it makes sense with the lyrics.

JINGLE BELLS

Words and Music by J. Pierpont

LESSON 6:

Eighth Notes

An *eighth note* receives half a beat of sound. Often, they are paired in groups of two. Two or more eighth notes have a beam across the stems. A single eighth note has a flag. To count eighth notes we must subdivide the beat. We use the word "and" to do this. So, a group of eighth notes would be counted as "one-&-two-&-three-&-four-&" (& = and).

New Note: A

SKIP TO MY LOU

Traditional

TOOLBOX

Repeat Sign

A *repeat sign* is a symbol that indicates a section should be repeated. If the piece has one repeat sign alone, repeat from the very beginning.

WE ARE FAMILY

Words and Music by Nile Rodgers and Bernard Edwards

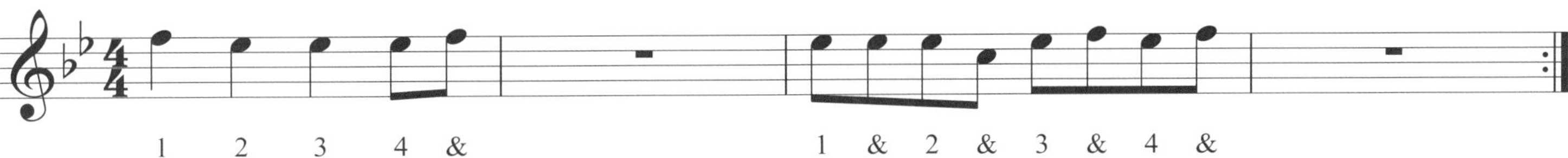

TOOLBOX

Dynamics

Dynamics indicate how loud or soft to play the music.

Softest ◄--► Loudest

Symbol:	*pp*	*p*	*mp*	*mf*	*f*	*ff*
Italian:	Pianissimo	Piano	Mezzo Piano	Mezzo Forte	Forte	Fortissimo
English:	Very Soft	Soft	Medium Soft	Medium Loud	Loud	Very Loud

Remember to use full breath support to control your tone at all dynamic levels. Successful dynamic contrast is achieved best when you can control your airstream using your abdomen. When practicing, experiment with how loud and soft you can play. As you gain proficiency on your instrument your dynamic range will grow.

ODE TO JOY

Words by Henry van Dyke • Music by Ludwig van Beethoven

TOOLBOX

Tie

A *tie* is a curved line connecting notes of the *same* pitch. Play one note for the combined counts of the tied notes. For example, a half note tied to a quarter note is held for three beats. You will only tongue the first note in a tie.

ALOUETTE

Traditional

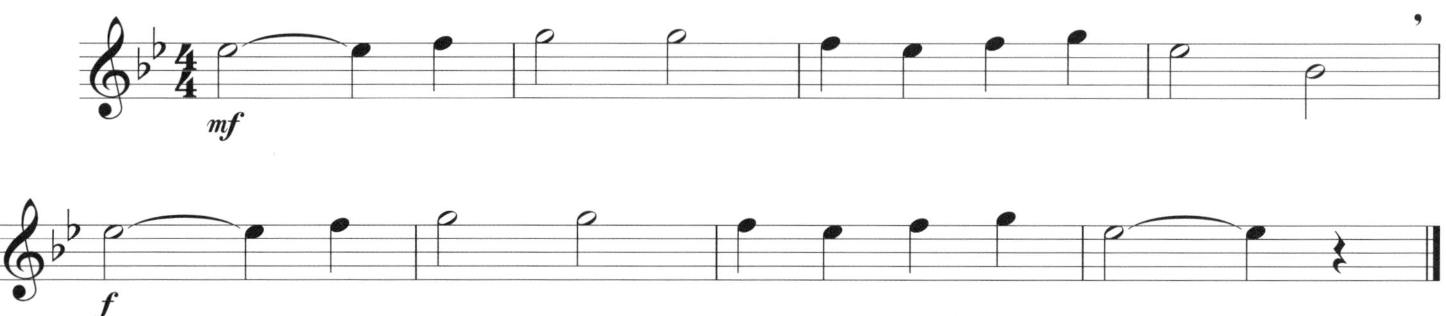

TOOLBOX

Ties Over the Measure

Ties over the measure are treated the same as ties within the same measure. Play one note for the combined counts of the tied notes, tonguing only once. In the next exercise, the tie extends over two measures. This first happens in measures two and three. The tie connects a quarter note (one beat) to a whole note (four beats). This means the tie receives a total of five beats.

LEAN ON ME

Words and Music by Bill Withers

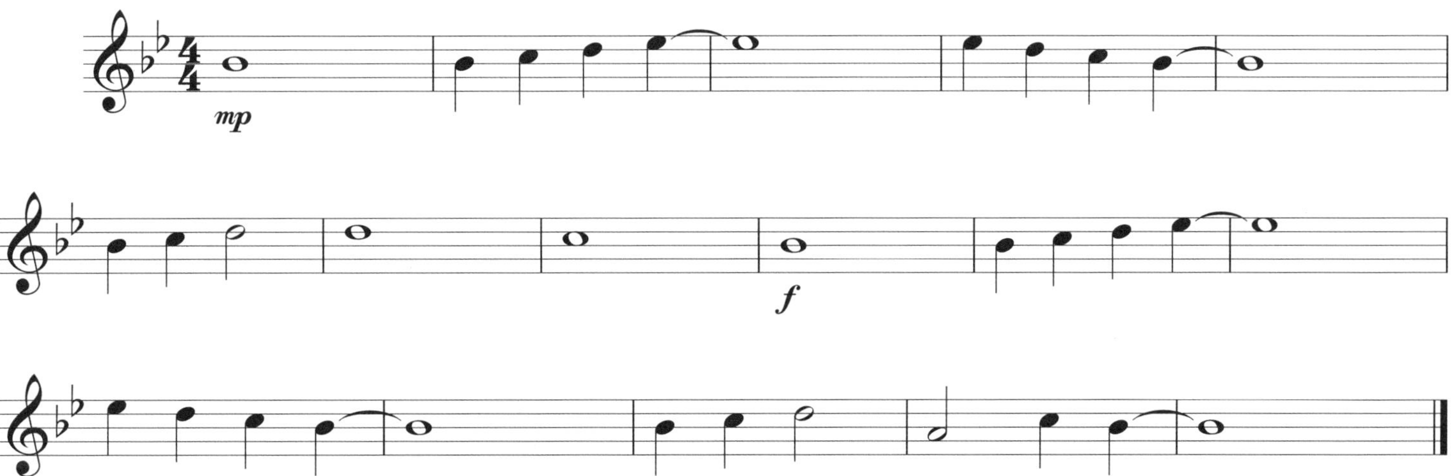

TOOLBOX

Dotted Notes

A dot adds half the value of a note's length to the original duration. For example, a half note gets two beats, therefore, a dotted half note is worth three beats (a half note plus a quarter note).

𝅗𝅥 + ♩ = 𝅗𝅥.

You will notice in the melody below that it sounds the same as the "Alouette" played earlier. In music, there are oftentimes more than one way to write something.

ALOUETTE – TAKE TWO

Traditional

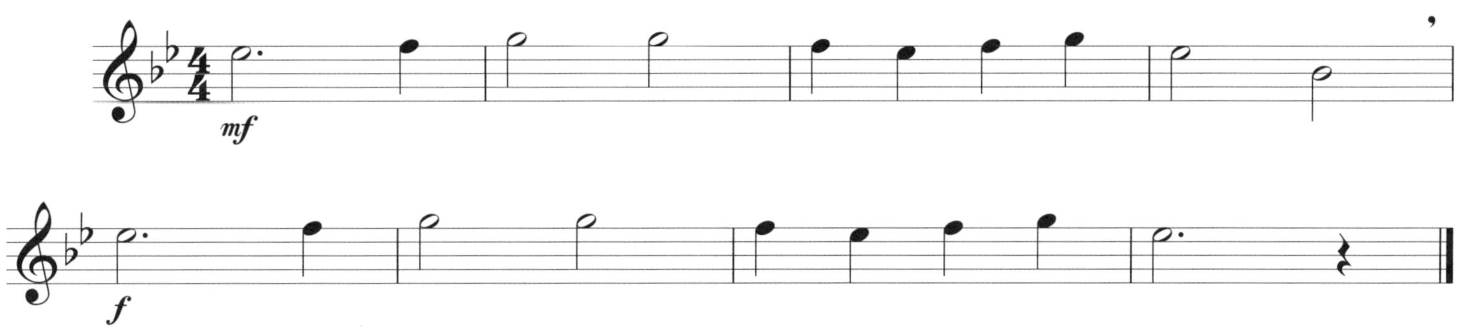

BLOWIN' IN THE WIND

Words and Music by Bob Dylan

mf

Eighth Rest 𝄾

An *eighth rest* gets half a beat of silence. Taking quick breaths during eighth rests will help you place the notes correctly.

New Note: Low G

> **TOOLBOX**
>
> **Playing Low Notes**
>
> In order to produce a beautiful sound in the low register of the flute, try using a lower angle of air, making more of an "oh" shape with your lips, and using warmer air.

SHUT UP AND DANCE

Words and Music by Ryan McMahon, Ben Berger, Sean Waugaman, Eli Maiman, Nicholas Petricca and Kevin Ray

Eighth Rest + Quarter Note

When encountering an eighth rest followed by a quarter note, make sure the quarter note's length is a full count. To feel the rhythm properly, take a quick breath and/or stomp your foot on the eighth rest.

BLISTER IN THE SUN

Words and Music by Gordon Gano

LESSON 7:
Analyzing Music

As we begin to learn more markings and symbols in our music, it is important to analyze what is in front of you instead of jumping right into playing. When learning a new song, scan through the music looking for any markings you are unfamiliar with. Also take note of the key signature, time signature, and any accidentals in the music.

Tempo Markings

Tempo is the speed of music. At the beginning of a piece, the tempo is indicated in the top left corner. Marked tempos are end goals; when first learning a melody, play it much slower than the marked tempo and gradually increase your speed as you feel comfortable.

TEMPO		
Italian	Definition	BPM (Beats per Minute)
Largo	Very slowly	♩ = 40-60
Adagio	Slowly	♩ = 60-80
Andante	Walking pace	♩ = 80-108
Moderato	Moderate	♩ = 108-120
Allegro	Fast	♩ = 120-156
Vivace	Very fast	♩ = 156-176
Presto	Very, very fast	♩ = 176 and up

THE LONGEST TIME

Words and Music by Billy Joel

SPRING
from THE FOUR SEASONS
By Antonio Vivaldi

$\frac{2}{4}$ Time Signature

REMINDER: A time signature determines how many beats are in each measure and what type of note gets one beat. The top number represents how many beats are in each measure, while the bottom number represents what kind of note receives one beat.

A 2/4 time signature has two beats per measure. The quarter note gets one beat.

FRÉRE JACQUES
Traditional

DOWN BY THE STATION

Traditional

$\frac{3}{4}$ Time Signature

A 3/4 time signature has three beats per measure. The quarter note gets one beat.

MORNING 

from PEER GYNT

By Edvard Grieg

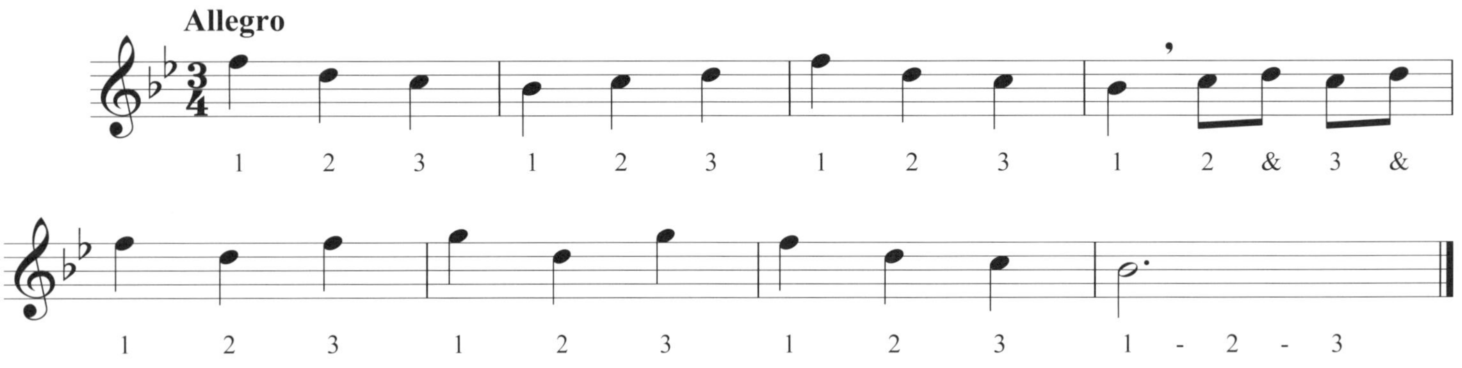

OPEN ARMS

Words and Music by Steve Perry and Jonathan Cain

Key of E-Flat

REMINDER: A key signature indicates whether to play a note sharp, flat, or natural. Flat ♭ or sharp ♯ signs are placed after the treble clef. The line or space that the sharp or flat occupies indicates which notes are changed.

This key signature has three flats: B-flat, E-flat, and A-flat.

New Note: High A-Flat

The fingering for A-flat adds the left-hand pinkie. Make sure your left-hand pinkie is always resting gently on the A-flat key. This will ensure it is ready to go at a moment's notice and will make playing the A-flat easier as your music becomes more challenging.

YANKEE DOODLE

Traditional

I LOVE ROCK 'N ROLL

Words and Music by Alan Merrill and Jake Hooker

THE MEDALLION CALLS

from PIRATES OF THE CARIBBEAN: THE CURSE OF THE BLACK PEARL

Music by Klaus Badelt

EVERY BREATH YOU TAKE

Music and Lyrics by Sting

TOOLBOX

Dotted Quarter Note + Eighth Note

Remember, a dot adds half the value of the note. So, a dotted quarter note is worth one and a half beats. A dotted quarter note followed by an eighth note is worth two beats.

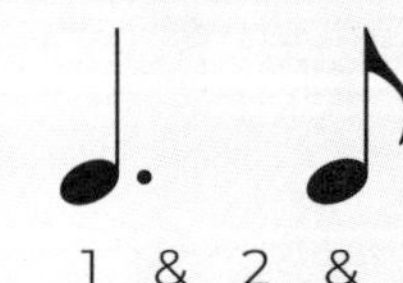

1 & 2 &

MY COUNTRY, 'TIS OF THEE (AMERICA)

Words by Samuel Francis Smith • Music from Thesaurus Musicus

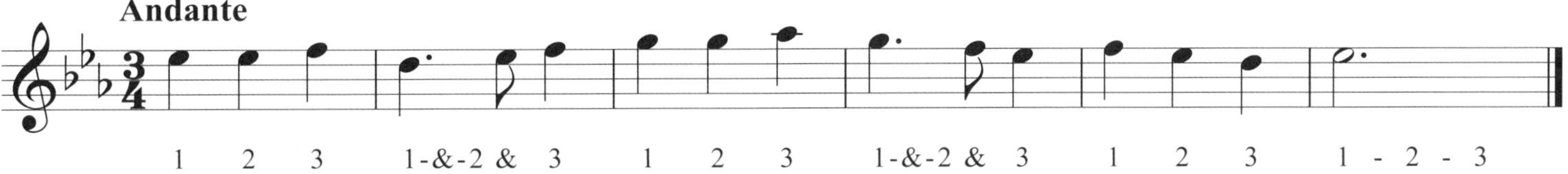

New Note: A-Flat

FLUTE TALK

Low and High Note Fingerings

Many notes on flute have the same fingering for the low note and high note. The A-flat is one such case. It is important to develop a flexible embouchure to easily adjust from low to high. Some notes on the flute have different fingerings in various octaves. When you encounter these, follow the fingerings printed in this book.

Here are a few tips for successful low notes:

- Use a lower angle of air.
- Make more of an "oh" shape with your lips.
- Create warmer, sometimes slower air.

Drill: A-Flat Octave Exercise

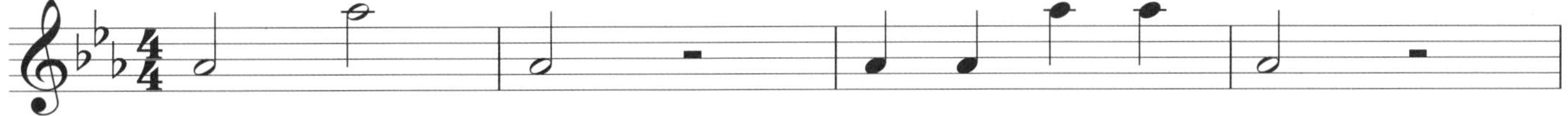

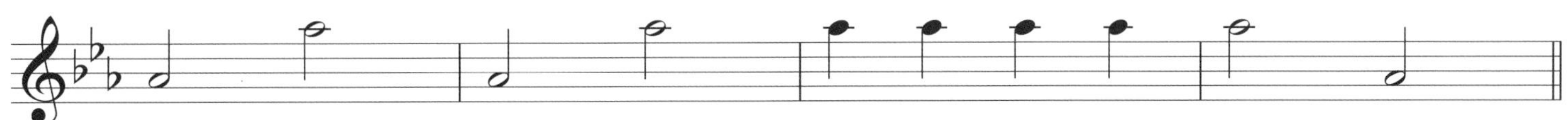

Key of A-Flat

This key signature has four flats: B flat, E flat, A-flat, and D-flat.

New Note: D-Flat

SHE DRIVES ME CRAZY

Words and Music by David Steele and Roland Gift

TOOLBOX

Longer Ties

Remember that a tie combines the value of notes together. When a tie is across more than two notes, tongue the note once and hold for the combined value. Starting in measure 6 of the melody below (we don't count the pick-up as a measure), there is tie that stretches over seven beats. Be certain of your counting in this section. Tap your foot and count in your head.

ON TOP OF OLD SMOKY

Kentucky Mountain Folksong

LESSON 8:
New Notes and Rhythms

In this lesson we'll learn several new notes. Be sure to use the correct fingerings and practice transitioning between notes using the down-up exercise explained in Lesson 4.

New Note: E

> **TOOLBOX**
>
> **Natural Sign ♮**
>
> A *natural sign* is a type of accidental that is used to cancel a sharp or flat note. "Natural" simply indicates that a note is not sharp or flat. For example, an "E-natural" is the same as an "E."

SMOKE ON THE WATER

Words and Music by Ritchie Blackmore, Ian Gillan, Roger Glover, Jon Lord and Ian Paice

New Note: High A

GHOSTBUSTERS

from the Columbia Motion Picture GHOSTBUSTERS

Words and Music by Ray Parker, Jr.

TRUE COLORS

Words and Music by Billy Steinberg and Tom Kelly

TOOLBOX

Eighth Note + Dotted Quarter Note

An eighth note followed by a dotted quarter note is worth two beats. In the next melody, this rhythmic combination occurs in the penultimate measure. It is counted as "3-&4&" or "short-long."

1 & 2 &

TOOLBOX

Courtesy Accidental

An accidental that is in parenthesis is called a *courtesy accidental* and serves as a reminder that a note is no longer sharp or flat.

I'M A BELIEVER

Words and Music by Neil Diamond

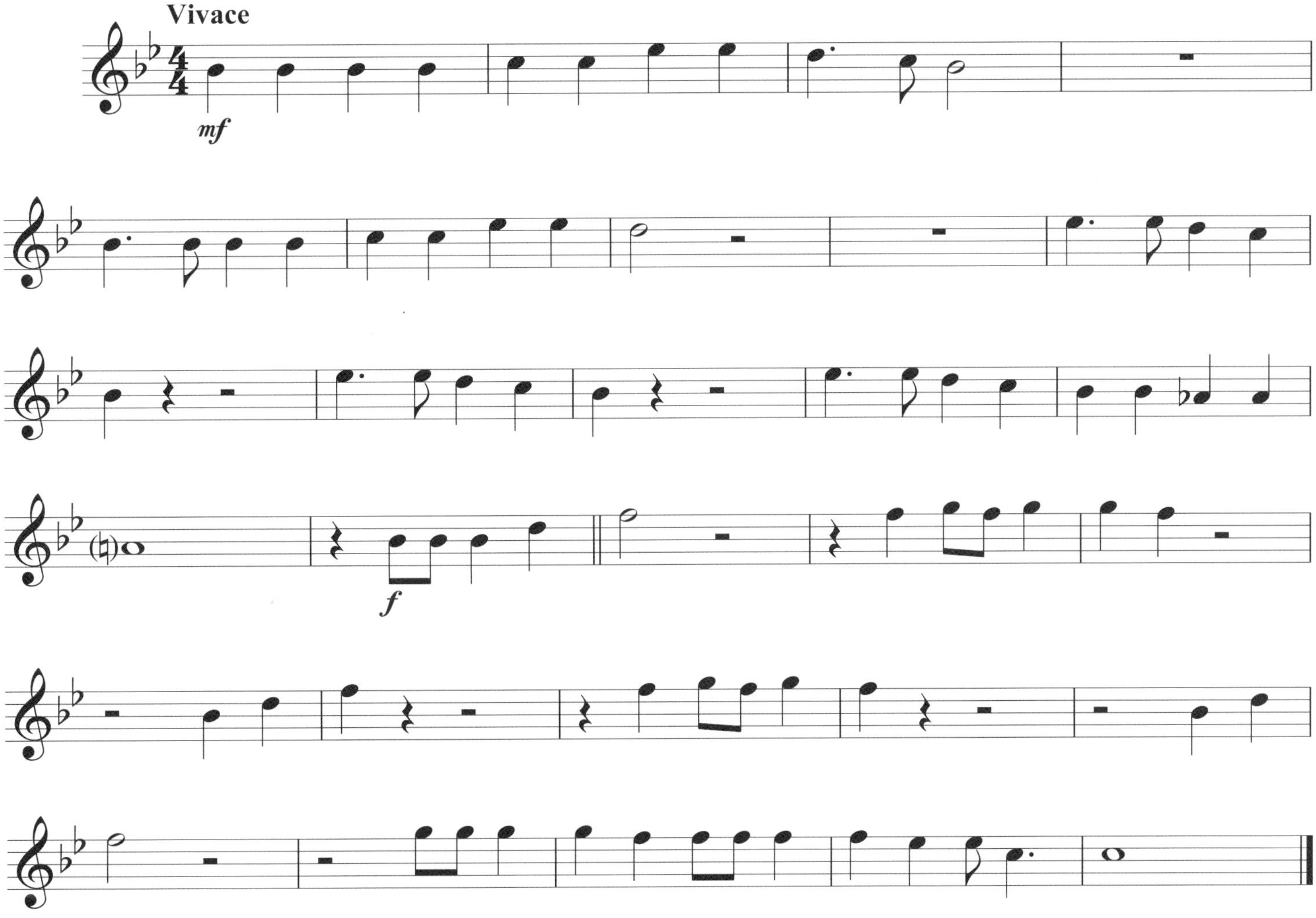

Vivace
mf
f

New Note: High B-Flat

SHEPHERD'S HEY

English Folk Song

Vivace
f

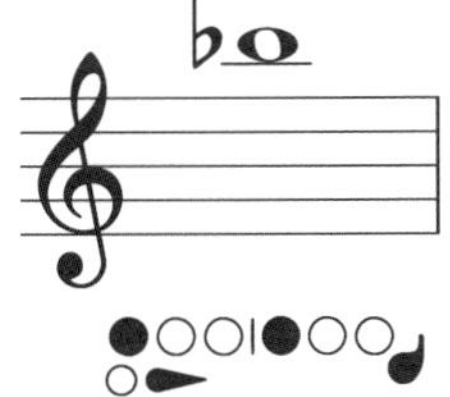

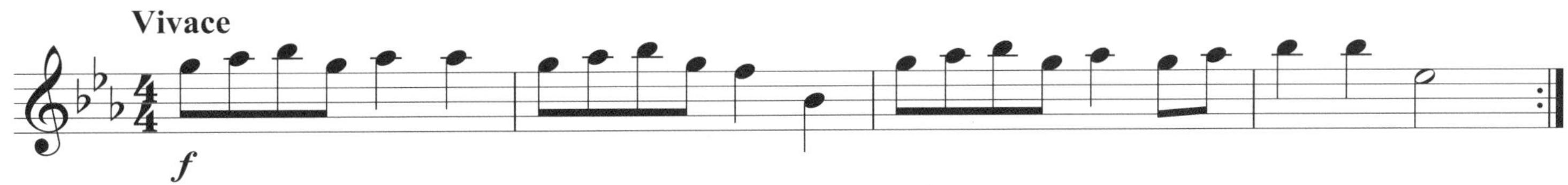

JOY TO THE WORLD

Words by Isaac Watts • Music by George Frideric Handel • Adapted by Lowell Mason

SUPERCALIFRAGILISTICEXPIALIDOCIOUS

from MARY POPPINS

Words and Music by Richard M. Sherman and Robert B. Sherman

New Note: Low F

THEME FROM "JURASSIC PARK"

from the Universal Motion Picture JURASSIC PARK

New Note: High G-Flat

(SITTIN' ON) THE DOCK OF THE BAY

Words and Music by Steve Cropper and Otis Redding

LESSON 9:
Warm-Ups and Intonation

Warm-Ups

Good musicians spend a great deal of time thoughtfully warming up their instruments. As flutists, playing long tones, scales, scale patterns, arpeggios, and lip slurs help our tone production, lip flexibility, and technical facility. Each time you play, take time to do a few warm-ups before diving into other aspects of flute playing. At first, play them slowly. As you become more comfortable with the material, try playing them at different tempos and even different articulations.

B-Flat Major Scale

Scales are the building blocks of most songs. They help the development of proper embouchure, air, and fingerings. All major scales sound the same but start on different notes with different key signatures. The B-flat major scale is one of the most common scales flute players learn. If a breath is needed, take one after the high B-flat.

Drill: B-Flat Major Scale

Drill: B-Flat Steps

TOOLBOX

Crescendo and Decrescendo

A *crescendo* means to gradually get louder. A *decrescendo* means to gradually get softer.

To play a successful crescendo or decrescendo, use of air is critical. Controlling air in the abdomen and pushing the correct amount at the proper time will yield the best result. Experiment with how loud and soft you can play over different lengths of time. Aim to always have a steady increase or decrease in volume.

AULD LANG SYNE

Words by Robert Burns · Traditional Scottish Melody

MY GIRL

Words and Music by Smokey Robinson and Ronald White

Long Tones

Long tones are great for getting warm air moving through your instrument and encourages good breath support from the moment you start playing. Maintain a steady beat and try adding a gradual crescendo and decrescendo on every note.

Drill: Long Tones

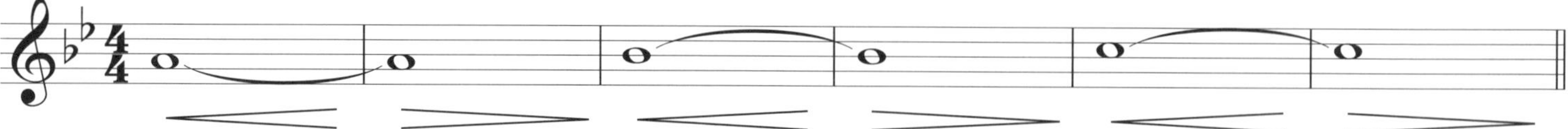

Intonation

Intonation refers to the accuracy of a pitch. It does not refer to whether you are playing the right note, but rather the exactness of that note.

Frequency

Pitch is measured as a unit of frequency known as hertz (symbol: Hz). A hertz is one cycle of a longitudinal sound wave per second. The human ear can perceive pitch in a range from 20 Hz to 20,000 Hz. In the United States, the accepted standard for tuning and manufacturing musical instruments is A=440 Hz (second space on the staff).

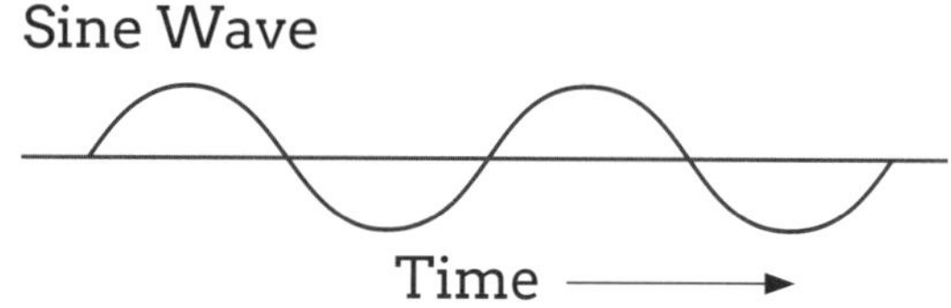

In Tune vs. Out of Tune

When two or more instruments play the same pitch but with non-matching frequencies, those pitches clash with each other. The result is an undesirable sound, and we say that they are "out of tune." For instance, if two instruments play the aforementioned "A," one at a frequency of 432 Hz and the other at a frequency of 449 Hz, they will not sound in tune. In contrast, when two or more instruments play at the same frequency it will sound as though only one instrument is playing; their pitches are a complete match.

Here's a more layman explanation of intonation:

- If two or more instruments play the same pitch and match, they are in tune and it sounds good.
- If they play the same pitch but do not quite match, they are out of tune and it does not sound good.

How to Tune the Flute

Tuning your flute is a matter of determining whether your pitch is too high (sharp) or too low (flat), and making necessary adjustments. Accomplishing this by ear is good practice and will develop your "musician ears." However, it is perfectly viable (in fact recommended) to use an electronic tuner. Tuners are readily available as an app for your smartphone or other device.

A tuner will show you whether you are sharp or flat, and is often measured in "cents." A cent is 1/100th of the smallest interval in music (a half-step). This gives you an idea of how small a cent of pitch is. An example of how musicians refer to cents is, "It sounds like I'm at least twenty cents flat."

1. Play a high A. You can play any note with a tuner, but A is a stable note for the flute.
2. If the tuner shows you are sharp, pull the headjoint out. This will lengthen your instrument and lower your pitch.
3. If the tuner shows you are flat, push the headjoint farther in. This will shorten your instrument and raise your pitch.
4. Use trial and error until the tuner shows that you are in tune.

What This Means for You

When you play alone, it is tempting to think that intonation doesn't matter. However, you will do well to tune every time you practice so that when it comes time to play with others (or a recording) you will know what to do. Playing in tune requires the reinforcement of habits that are essential to playing the flute, namely air support and embouchure.

LESSON 10:
Road Maps

Much like reading a road map, knowing how to read all signs and symbols in music helps musicians figure out where to go and what to do. There are a couple different symbols that indicate a musician is to repeat certain sections of music.

1st and 2nd Endings

Play through the 1st ending like a standard repeat sign and return to the beginning. On the second time through, skip the 1st ending and play the 2nd ending.

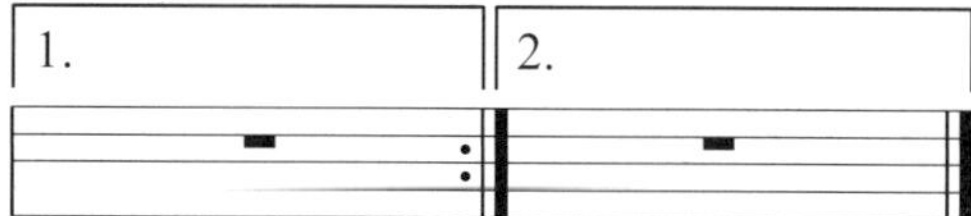

JOLLY OLD ST. NICHOLAS

Traditional 19th Century American Carol

ACHY BREAKY HEART (DON'T TELL MY HEART)

Words and Music by Don Von Tress

Dynamic Changes

When playing a march, it is common to play a different dynamic level on the repeat. This is marked by a hyphen between the two dynamics. This adds contrast and makes for a more interesting performance.

THE VICTORS (MICHIGAN FIGHT SONG)

By Louis Elbel

Forward Repeat Sign 𝄆

A *forward repeat sign* indicates a musician needs to go back to a specific spot in the music and repeat that section. If there is no forward repeat sign, musicians must go back to the beginning.

BAD ROMANCE

Words and Music by Stefani Germanotta and Nadir Khayat

D.C. al Fine

D.C. is the abbreviation for *Da Capo*, or "to the beginning." *Fine* (fee-nay) means "the end." At the D.C. al Fine, go back to the beginning, and stop playing at Fine.

THE BANANA BOAT SONG

Jamaican Work Song

LARGO

from THE NEW WORLD SYMPHONY

By Antonin Dvorak

Odd Repeats

Unless otherwise marked, repeats are generally observed only the first time through.

In "All Through the Night," the first four measures are marked as a repeat. But, with the D.C. al Fine, those four measures will also be played at the end. In this case, there's no need to repeat the first four measures when taking the D.C. al Fine.

ALL THROUGH THE NIGHT

Welsh Folksong

In "We're Not Gonna Take It," there is a D.C. al Fine at the second ending. After playing the repeat, return to the beginning of the piece and stop at Fine.

WE'RE NOT GONNA TAKE IT

Words and Music by Daniel Dee Snider

LESSON 11:
Articulations

Articulation refers to the many ways a note can be played. It is what gives the music its character and style.

Accent

An *accent* creates a heavy and separated sound. Accents require a surge of a little more air. Be careful not to use more tongue, as that can diminish the resonant sound of the actual pitch of the note. Once you feel comfortable with this technique, feel free to add accents to other melodies you have already played in this book.

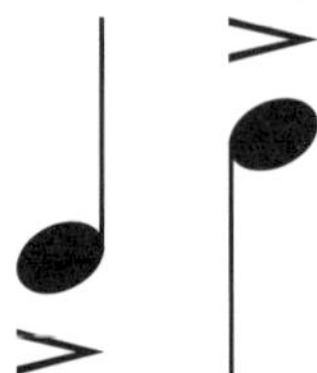

CHIAPANECAS (MEXICAN CLAPPING SONG)

Mexican Folk Song

AMERICA

from WEST SIDE STORY

Lyrics by Stephen Sondheim · Music by Leonard Bernstein

MONY, MONY

Words and Music by Bobby Bloom, Tommy James, Ritchie Cordell and Bo Gentry

Staccato

A *staccato* is a light and separated sound and requires a lighter touch of the tongue inside your mouth. It creates a bouncier sound and can be thought of as a tip toe for your tongue. Once you feel comfortable with this technique, feel free to add staccatos to other melodies you have already played in this book.

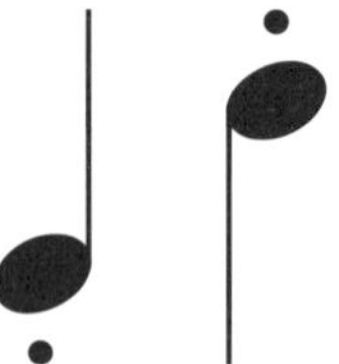

THIS IS HALLOWEEN

from THE NIGHTMARE BEFORE CHRISTMAS

Music and Lyrics by Danny Elfman

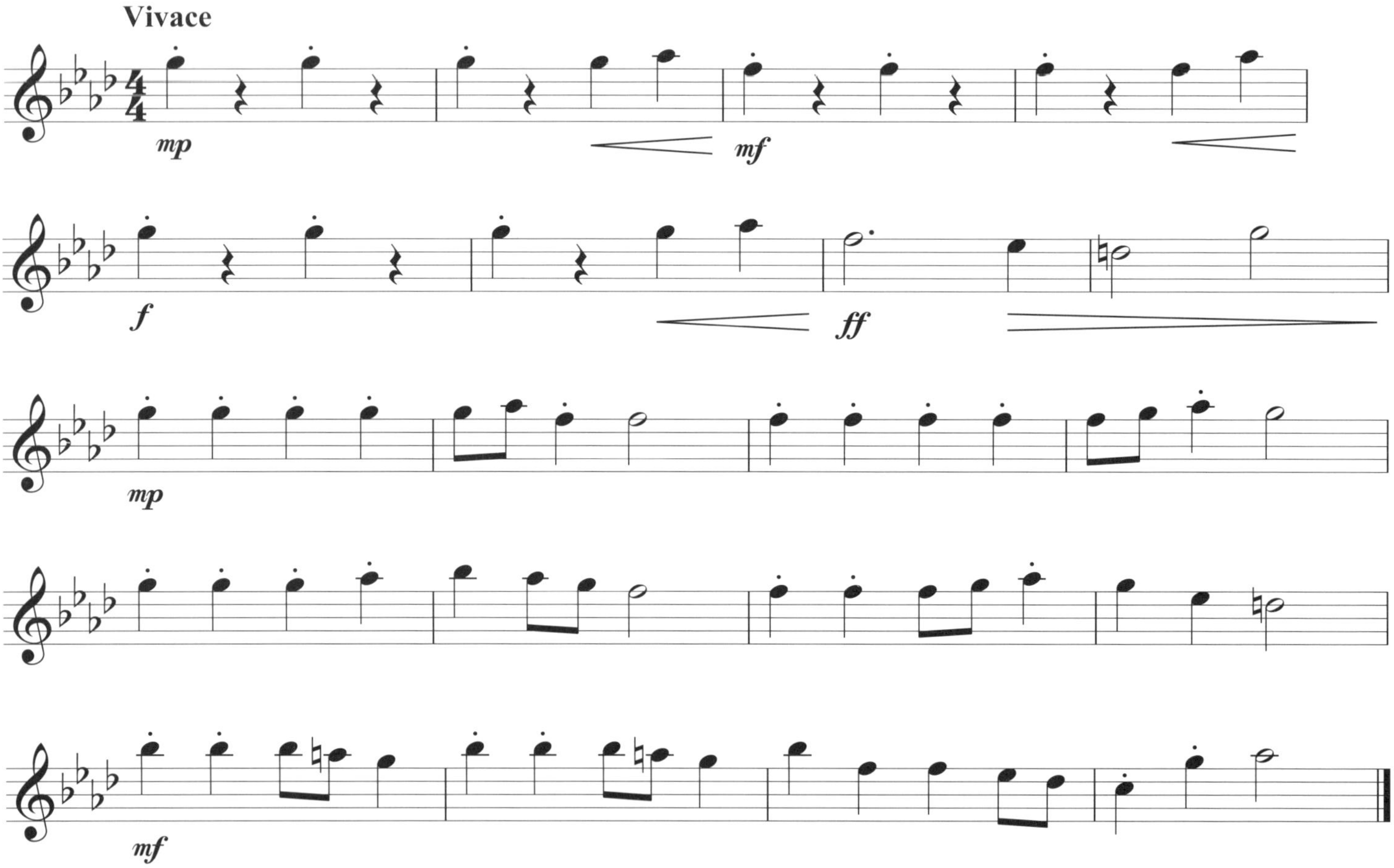
Vivace
mp
mf
f
ff
mp
mf

SUNSHINE OF YOUR LOVE

Words and Music by Eric Clapton, Jack Bruce and Pete Brown

Moderato
f

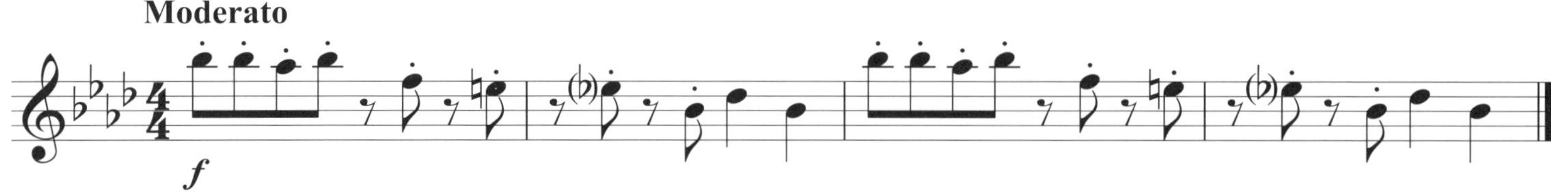

Swing Eighths

Swing eighths is a type of rhythmic feel. In a pair of eighth notes, the first note will last a little longer than the second. So, in a set of four eighth notes, it will sound, "long-short-long-short." This concept is best learned by listening. Make sure you watch the corresponding video.

HAPPY BIRTHDAY TO YOU

Words and Music by Mildred J. Hill and Patty S. Hill

ISN'T SHE LOVELY

Words and Music by Stevie Wonder

New Note: B

HAPPY TOGETHER

Words and Music by Garry Bonner and Alan Gordon

Slur

A *slur* is a curved line that connects two or more notes of *different* pitch. Tongue only the first note in a slur. When playing a slur, it is important to push air between your notes, and to keep your air moving at a consistent speed.

LULLABY

By Johannes Brahms

THE BLUE BELLS OF SCOTLAND

Words and Music attributed to Mrs. Jordon

TOOLBOX

Building Technical Facility

Practice exercises like thirds and scale patterns in the other keys you've learned (e.g., F Major). Memorizing these exercises and being able to play them in any key will greatly improve technical facility on your instrument. As you continue to improve, challenge yourself with adding in different articulation patterns. Here's a couple to get you started:

Two Tongue, Two Slur

Two Slur, Two Tongue

One Tongue, Three Slur

New Note: High C

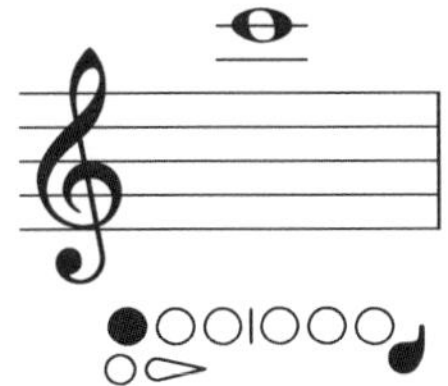

Drill: B-Flat Major Thirds

TOMORROW

from the Musical Production ANNIE

Lyric by Martin Charnin • Music by Charles Strouse

FLUTE TALK

Low to High Notes

A challenge on flute is going from low notes to high notes, and vice versa. An exercise that can help with this is octave lip slurs. For example, slurring from a low B-flat to a high B-flat. This can be done in a variety of ways. Watch the video and try the exercise below to get you started and feel free to create your own.

Drill: Octave Slurs

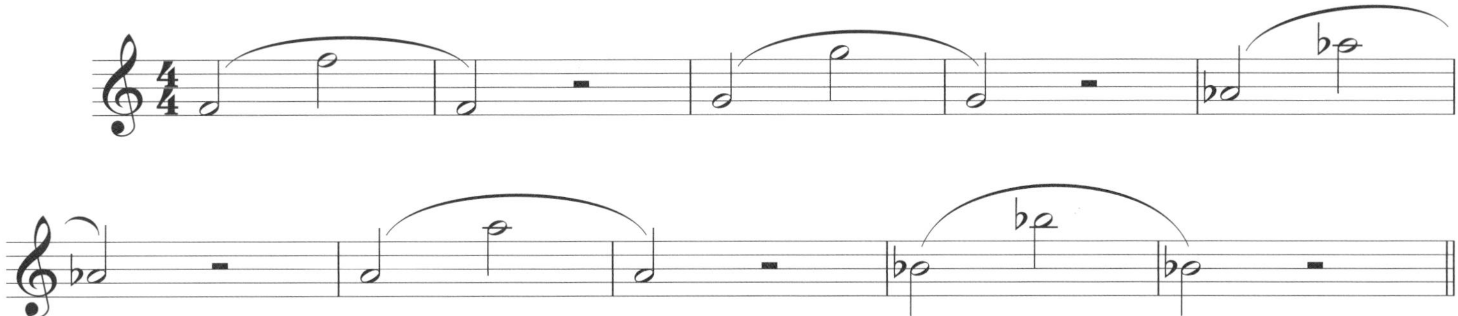

OVER THE RAINBOW

from THE WIZARD OF OZ

Music by Harold Arlen • Lyric by E.Y. "Yip" Harburg

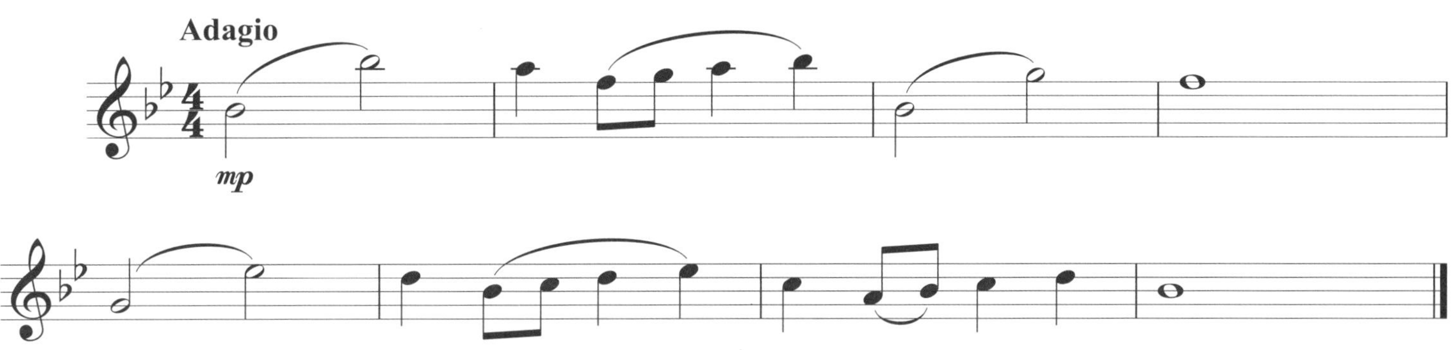

Tenuto

A *tenuto* sounds smooth and connected, with no break of sound between notes. It is marked as a line above or below a note head. Play the note for its full length.

DANNY BOY

Words by Frederick Edward Weatherly • Traditional Irish Folk Melody

IRON MAN

Words and Music by Frank Iommi, John Osbourne, William Ward and Terence Butler

FLUTE TALK

Even Sound

As you continue to improve, strive for an even sound in all registers of the flute. In the following melody, practice pushing your air between notes. When in doubt, use more air! Playing the flute takes as much air as playing a tuba. No wonder it is hard!

CARNIVAL OF VENICE

By Julius Benedict

O CANADA!

By Calixa Lavallee, l'Hon. Judge Routhier and Justice R.S. Weir

Andante

EINE KLEINE NACHTMUSIK

By Wolfgang Amadeus Mozart

LESSON 12:

Tempo Changes and Triplets

Fermata 𝄐

A *fermata* is a symbol that indicates a note or rest should be played longer than marked. If playing with an ensemble, hold the note as the conductor instructs.

KUM BA YAH

Traditional Spiritual

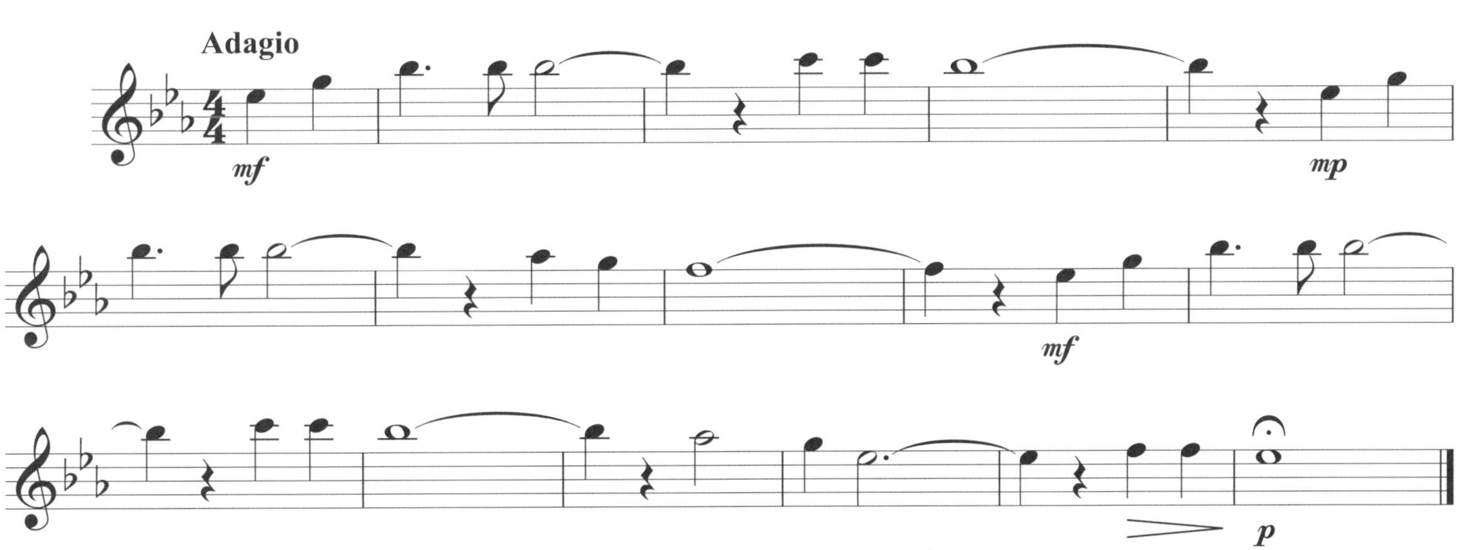

FORREST GUMP - MAIN TITLE (FEATHER THEME)

from the Paramount Motion Picture FORREST GUMP
Music by Alan Silvestri

Rallentando and Ritardando

Rallentando (*rall.*) and *ritardando* (*rit.*) are musical terms meaning to gradually get slower.

EDELWEISS

from THE SOUND OF MUSIC

Lyrics by Oscar Hammerstein II • Music by Richard Rodgers

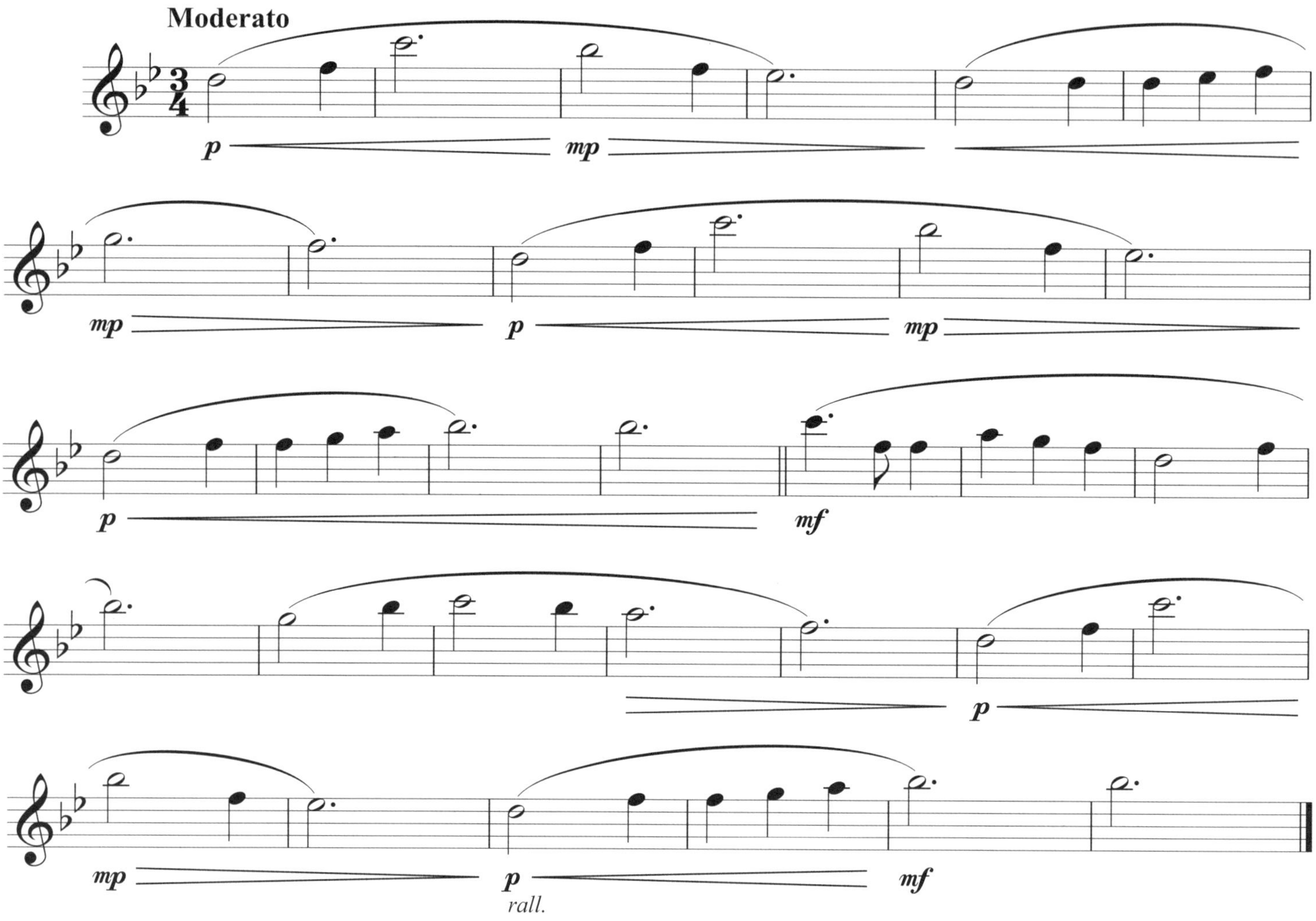
Moderato
p
mp
mp
p
mp
p
mf
p
mp
p
rall.
mf

Accelerando

An *accelerando* (*accel.*) means to gradually get faster.

CAN CAN

from ORPHEUS IN THE UNDERWORLD

By Jacques Offenbach

Allegro
mf
accel.

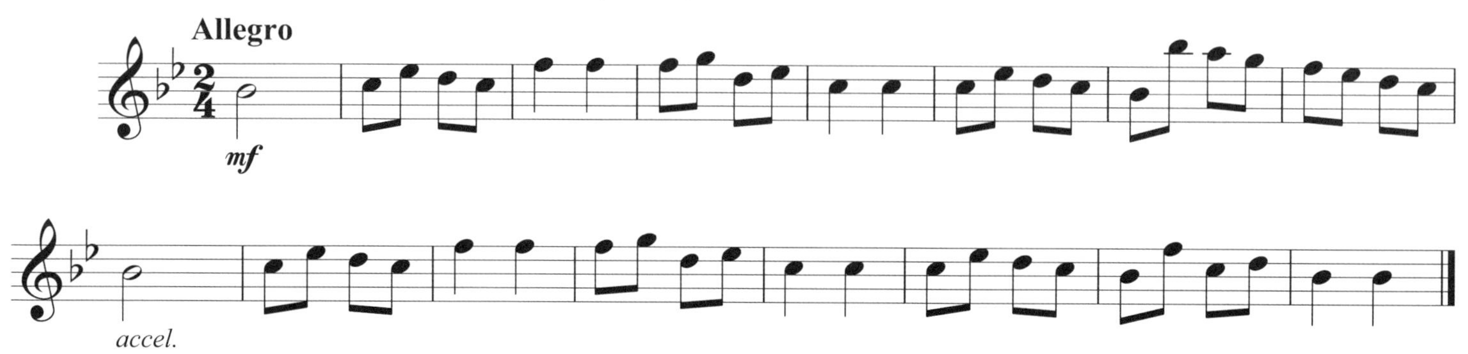

a tempo

The term *a tempo* means to go back to the previous tempo.

THAT'S AMORE (THAT'S LOVE)

from the Paramount Picture THE CADDY

Words by Jack Brooks • Music by Harry Warren

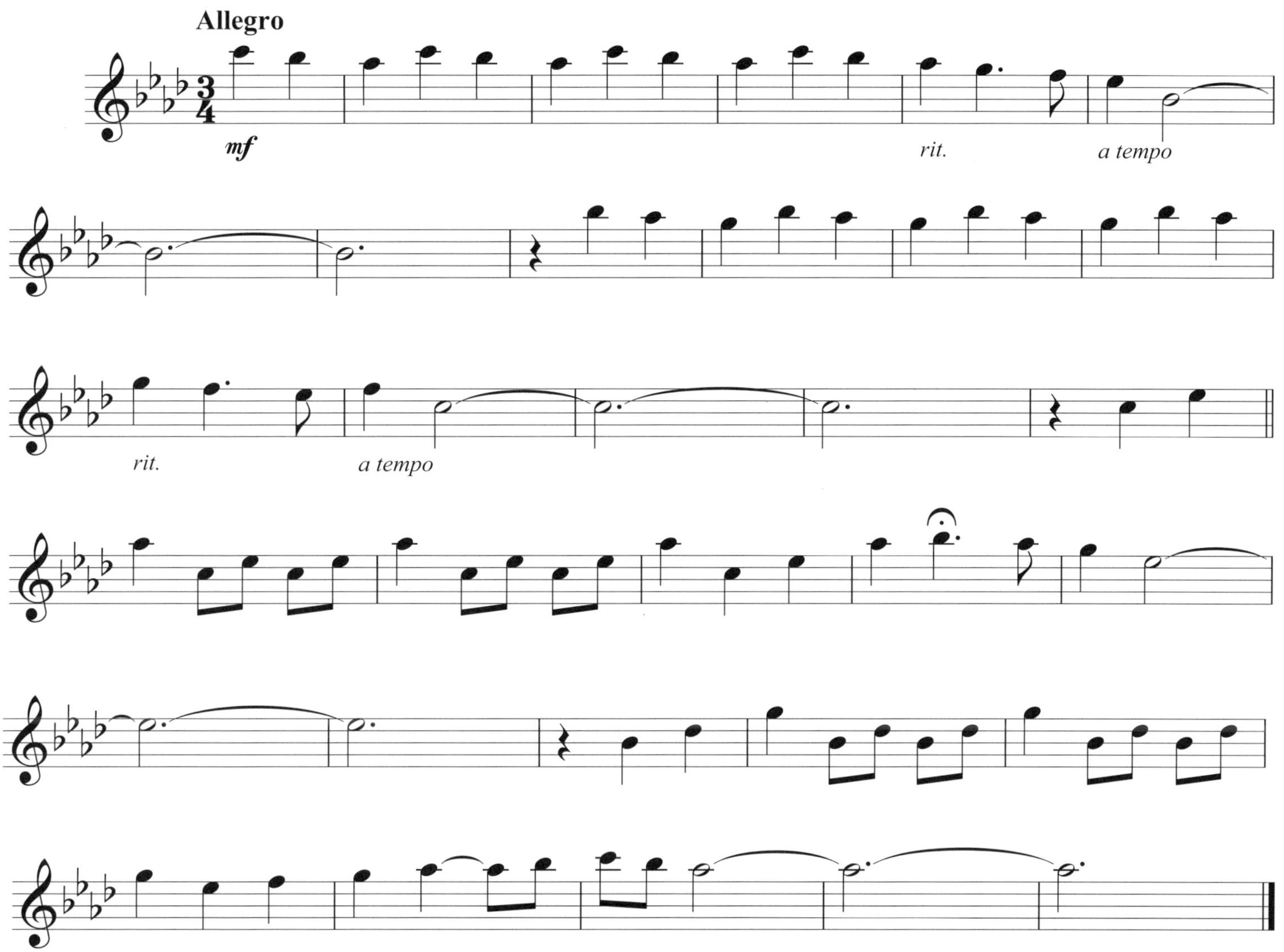

Triplets

A *triplet* is a group of three notes indicated by a "3" above or below the grouping. The most common types of triplets are quarter and eighth note triplets.

Three eighth note triplets fit into *one* beat. They can be counted as "one-trip-let, two-trip-let, three-trip-let, four-trip-let."

Three quarter note triplets fit into *two* beats. This is a bit more complex, as the musician must feel three notes fitting into two beats.

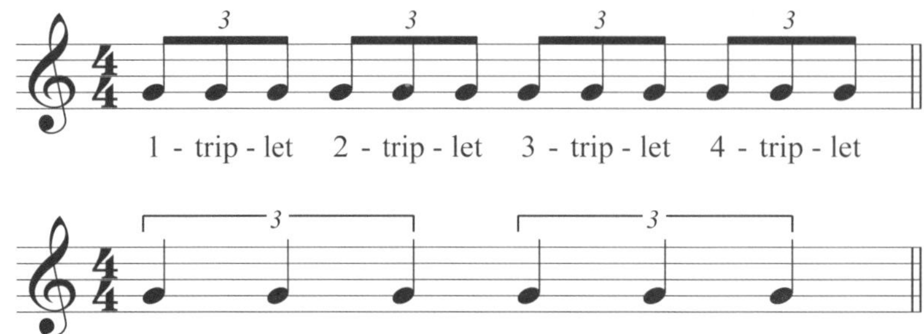

Drill: Eighth Note Triplets

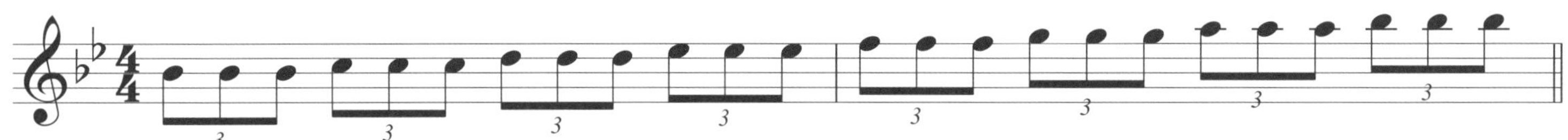

Drill: Quarter Note Triplets

SPONGEBOB SQUAREPANTS THEME SONG

from SPONGEBOB SQUAREPANTS

Words and Music by Mark Harrison, Blaise Smith, Stephen M. Hillenburg and Derek Drymon

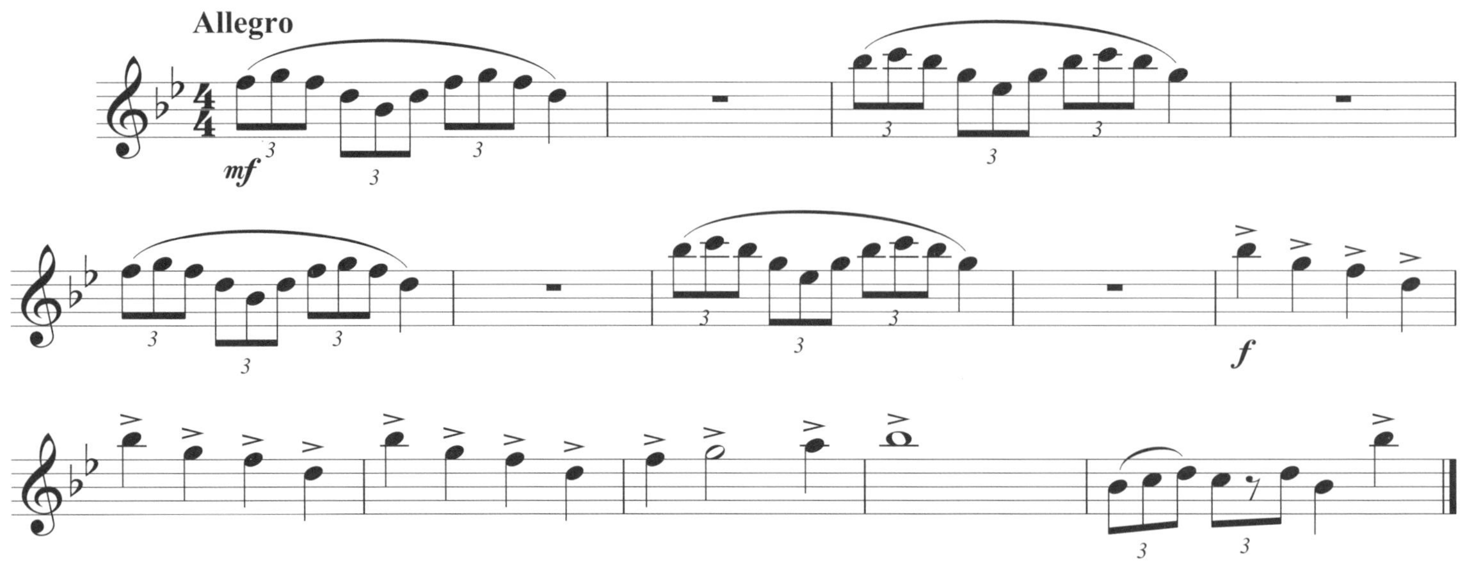

I'LL BE THERE

Words and Music by Berry Gordy Jr., Hal Davis, Willie Hutch and Bob West

CHARIOTS OF FIRE

from the Feature Film CHARIOTS OF FIRE

By Vangelis

Allegro

mf

1.

2.

f

ADDAMS FAMILY THEME

Theme from the TV Show and Movie

Music and Lyrics by Vic Mizzy

Moderato
f

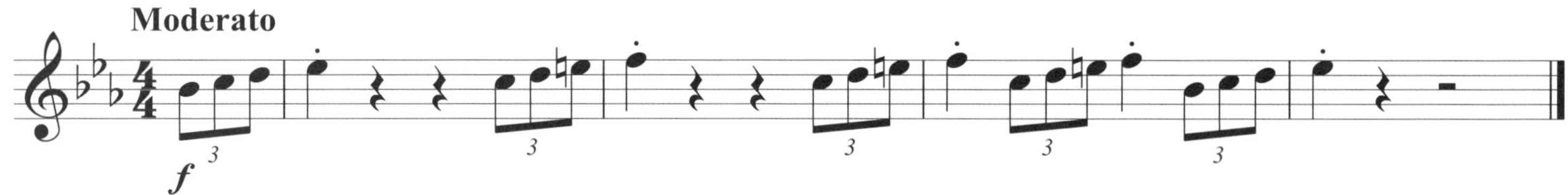

TOOLBOX

Triplets and Swing

Another way to think about swing eighths is that the two eighth notes are played as the first and third notes of an eighth note triplet set.

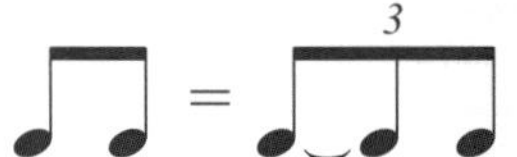

UNFORGETTABLE

Words and Music by Irving Gordon

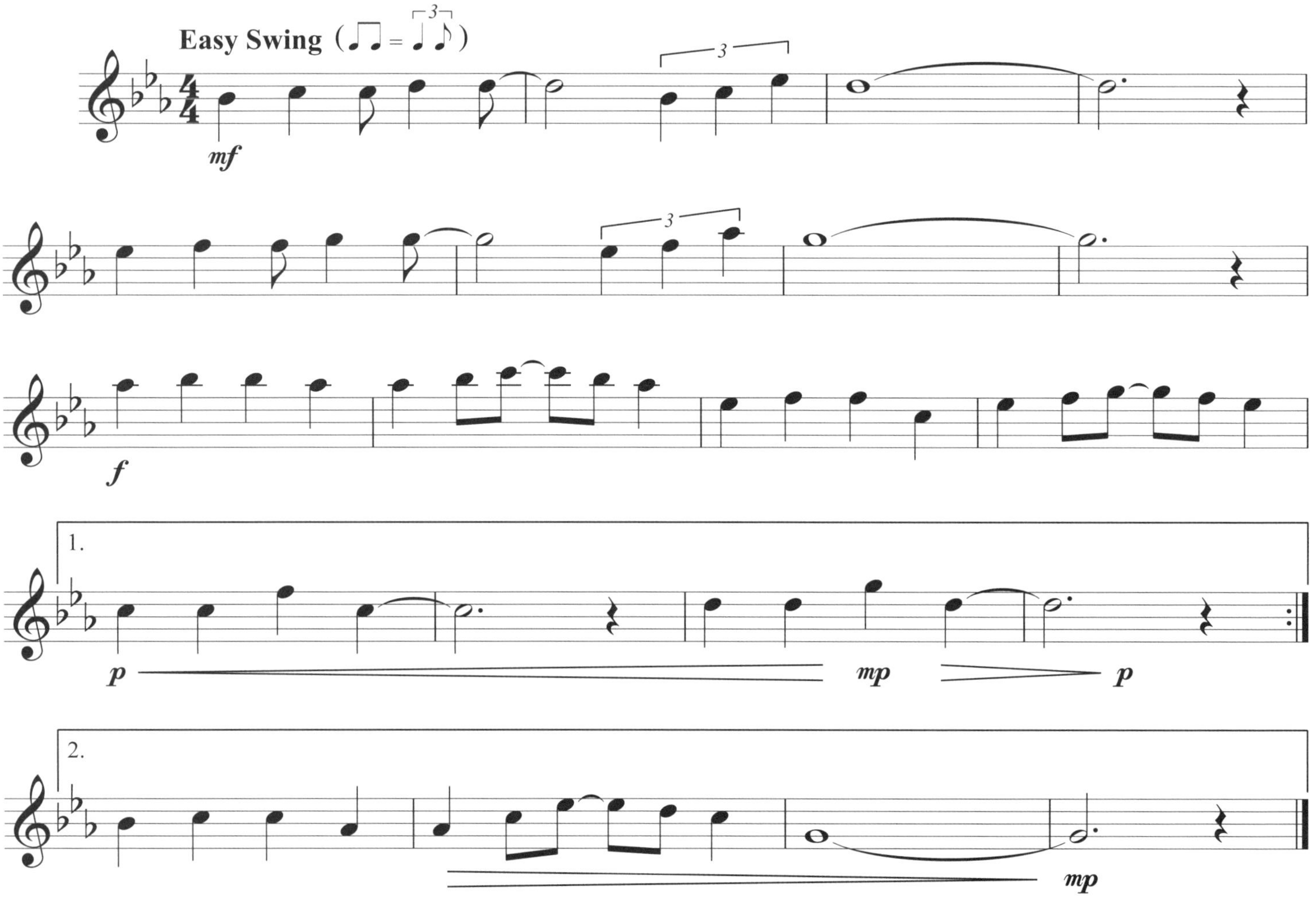
Easy Swing
mf
f
1.
p
mp
p
2.
mp

LESSON 13:
Exploring Key Signatures

Key of C

This key signature has NO sharps or flats. Everything is played natural, unless indicated by accidentals.

New Note: High B

LA CUCARACHA

Mexican Revolutionary Folksong

Allegro

mf

1.

2.

MR. TAMBOURINE MAN

Words and Music by Bob Dylan

New Note: High D

FLUTE TALK

High D

When played correctly, a high D sounds vibrant and clear. Make sure you use the correct fingering. Many beginning flute players will try to get by with the D fingering they are used to and over blowing to get the higher D out. While this can be achieved somewhat successfully, it does not sound like a D played with the intended fingering.

CAN'T HELP FALLING IN LOVE

Words and Music by George David Weiss, Hugo Peretti and Luigi Creatore

Key of F

This key signature has one flat: B-flat.

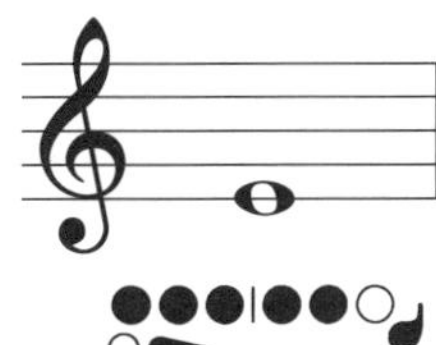

WE FOUND LOVE

Words and Music by Calvin Harris

MY HEART WILL GO ON (LOVE THEME FROM 'TITANIC')

from the Paramount and Twentieth Century Fox Motion Picture TITANIC

Music by James Horner • Lyric by Will Jennings

Key of G

This key signature has one sharp: F-sharp.

New Note: Low F-Sharp

New Note: F-Sharp

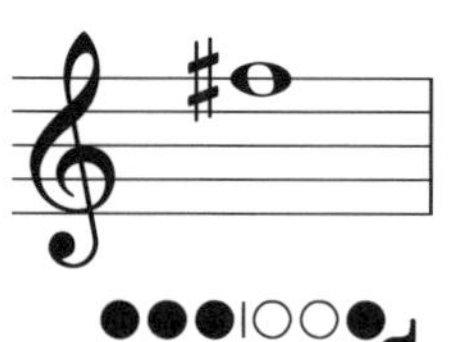

MINUET IN G

from NOTEBOOK FOR ANNA MAGDALENA BACH

By Christian Petzold

MY FAVORITE THINGS

from THE SOUND OF MUSIC

Lyrics by Oscar Hammerstein II • Music by Richard Rodgers

Presto

mf

f

LESSON 14:
Chromatics and Enharmonics

REVIEW

A half-step is the smallest interval (distance) between two notes. A note is altered by one half-step the following three ways:

FLAT
Lowers a note one half-step

SHARP
Raises a note one half-step

NATURAL
Cancels a sharp or flat

CHROMATIC

Chromatic generally refers to notes outside of a given key signature, which are displayed using the above symbols. The word chromatic comes from the Greek word khrōmatikos which means "relating to color." We use the word outside of music to mean very colorful, or having a sensation of colorful phenomenon. Just as a variety of colors add visual interest, chromatic notes add interest to music.

ENHARMONIC

The piano keyboard is a useful illustration for studying notes. Music ascends in pitch from left to right, and descends in pitch from right to left. Every adjacent note is one half-step apart. Two half-steps is one *whole-step*.

Every pitch has two names. For instance, the black key between C and D is arrived at by either raising the C or lowering the D. The resulting C♯ and a D♭ are *enharmonic* to each other; they are the same note.

There are two sets of white keys that have no black key in between: E to F, and B to C. These notes are already one half-step apart and contain enharmonic spellings as well, although you won't encounter them as often: E♯ and F, F♭ and E, B♯ and C, C♭ and B.

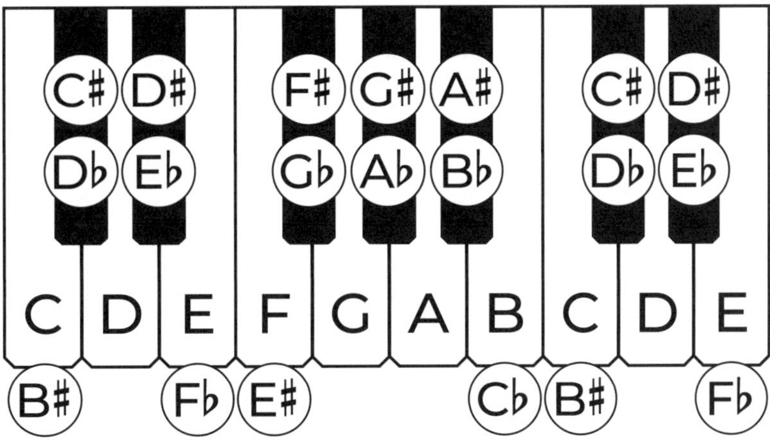

QUIZ

Here are few questions to check your understanding:

1. What note is enharmonic to an A♭?
2. What note is one half-step below E?
3. What note is one whole-step above B (remember: a whole-step is two half-steps)?
4. What note is one half-step above F♯?

Answers: 1. G♯ 2. E♭ or D♯ 3. C♯ or D♭ 4. G

The song "Greensleeves" has a C♯. Remember your enharmonic spellings, a C♯ is the same as a D♭.

GREENSLEEVES

Sixteenth Century Traditional English

Moderato

mf

f

CHROMATIC SCALE

A chromatic scale is made entirely of half-steps. This one-octave chromatic scale beginning on C will familiarize you with most of the fingerings on your flute and acquaint you with enharmonic spellings. Ascending notes are spelled with sharps and descending notes with flats. You will use the same fingerings both ways.

You have already encountered these notes in the book to this point. However, you have not yet encountered all enharmonic spellings. For example, when you see A♯, it is the same note as B♭.

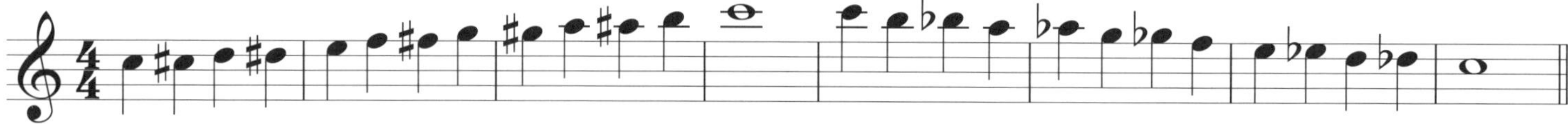

"Habanera" uses a portion of the chromatic scale. Enharmonic spellings are used.

HABANERA

from CARMEN

By GEORGES BIZET

Moderato

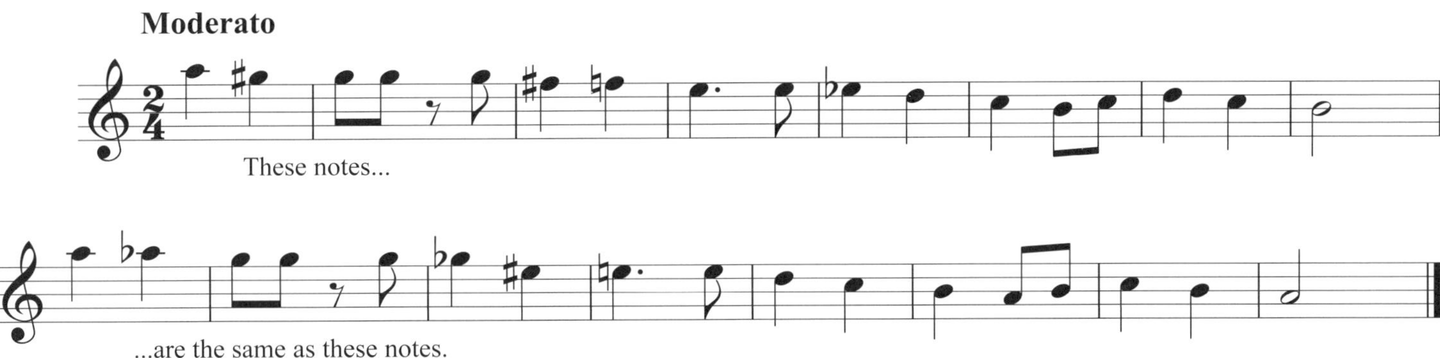

RONDO ALLA TURCA

from SONATA NO. 16 K. 331

By Wolfgang Amadeus Mozart

Allegro

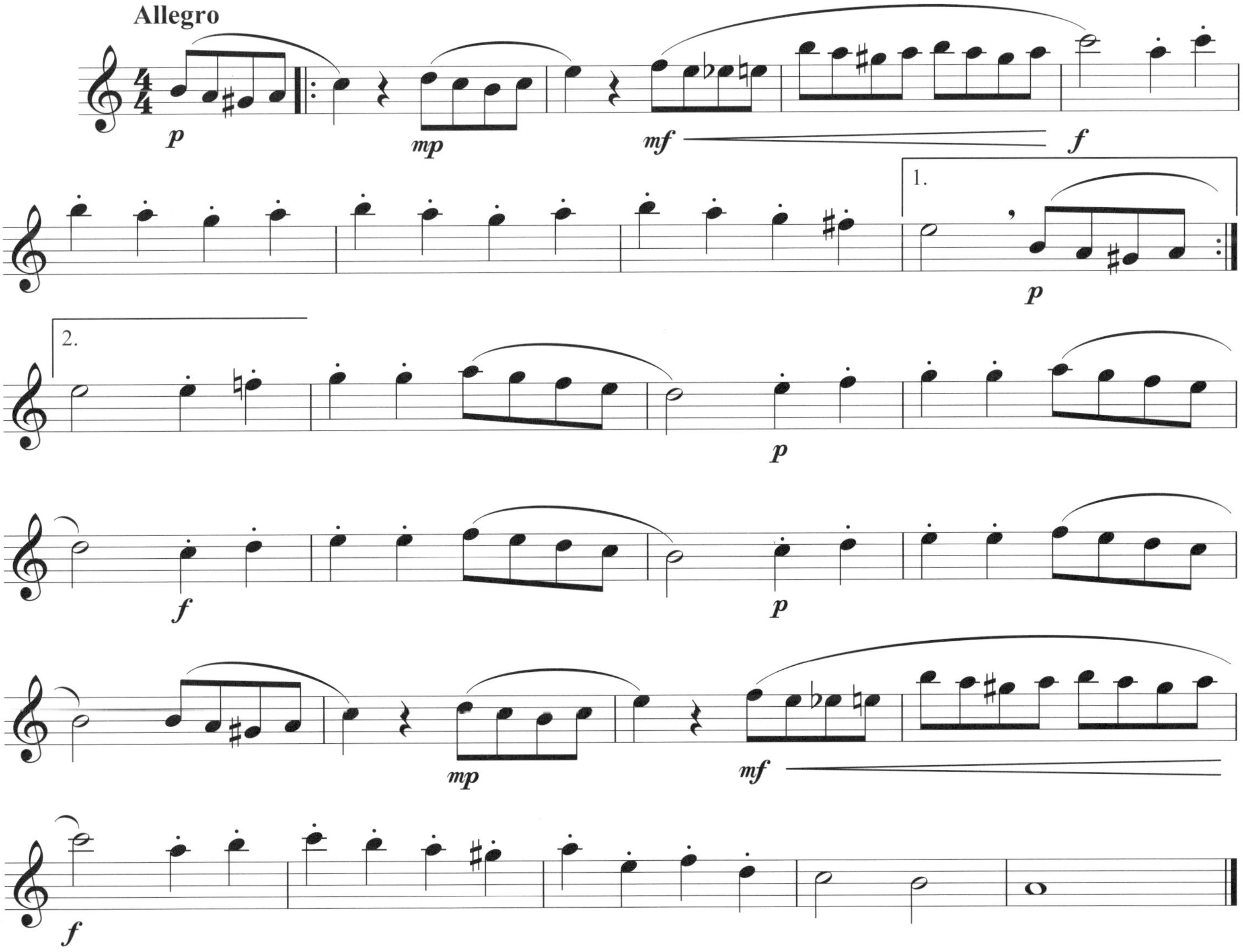

LESSON 15:
Practice Songs

Practicing the flute is rewarding, but it is not always easy, and it is normal to have highs and lows. Oftentimes it is exciting and fun, while other times it can be challenging or even frustrating. To gain the skills necessary to be a competent flute player, it is important to work through the highs and lows of practicing. Here are some practice tips:

- Think *consistency.* Daily practice for 15-20 minutes is a lot more desirable than hours once or twice a week. You are developing fundamentals. When you practice these fundamentals consistently, you are gaining the necessary muscle memory to make you feel comfortable and confident.
- Location, location, location. Designate a space in your home for practicing. This may be an office, a bedroom or other space that can always be at your disposal.
- Slow is the way to go. Begin each practice session with long tones. This can be done by finding slower, longer note examples in this book, or by simply practicing a scale in whole notes. As you play long tones, listen to your sound, and adjust as necessary to create a well-supported, resonant tone.
- Scales for technique. Utilize scales and scale patterns (arpeggios, thirds, etc.) to improve technique. The more you play certain patterns, the easier it becomes.
- Chunking. Isolate tricky passages or spots in your music. You can isolate as much or as little as you need. That may mean isolating a measure or two. It can also mean isolating just a couple of notes. Practicing only the isolated spot(s) is a lot more beneficial than playing an entire song repeatedly.
- Rule of threes. When isolating a section of music, play the isolated area three times slowly. Move on to something else and then come back to the isolated area and play it three more times (you can repeat this cycle as necessary over days and weeks). This helps with retention and muscle memory. As you become more comfortable with a section of music, gradually increase speed to the appropriate tempo.

> TOOLBOX
>
> **Metronome**
>
> A metronome is a tool that provides an audible beat such as a click sound, and a visible beat such as a pulsing flash. They can be easily found as an app for your phone or other device. Practicing with a metronome is an excellent way to maintain rhythmic accuracy and develop a strong internal pulse. A metronome uses a measurement called beats-per-minute (BPM), often expressed as quarter notes per minute. Choose a comfortable BPM that allows you to play accurately. A recommended starting point is ♩=80.

THE WANDERER

Words and Music by Ernest Maresca

WILLIAM TELL OVERTURE

By Gioachino Rossini

25 OR 6 TO 4

Words and Music by Robert Lamm

TOOLBOX

Feeling $\frac{3}{4}$ in 1

When songs have a quicker tempo in 3/4 we often refer to the tempo as being felt in one. So, instead of three beats per measure there is one. Set your metronome at a speed where each click equals a dotted half note. When playing, place a greater emphasis on the first beat of each measure.

PIANO MAN

Words and Music by Billy Joel

OH, PRETTY WOMAN

Words and Music by Roy Orbison and Bill Dees

DO-RE-MI

from THE SOUND OF MUSIC

Lyrics by Oscar Hammerstein II · Music by Richard Rodgers

YOU ARE MY SUNSHINE

Words and Music by Jimmie Davis

HEART AND SOUL

from the Paramount Short Subject A SONG IS BORN

Words by Frank Loesser · Music by Hoagy Carmichael

STRANGERS IN THE NIGHT

adapted from A MAN COULD GET KILLED

Words by Charles Singleton and Eddie Snyder · Music by Bert Kaempfert

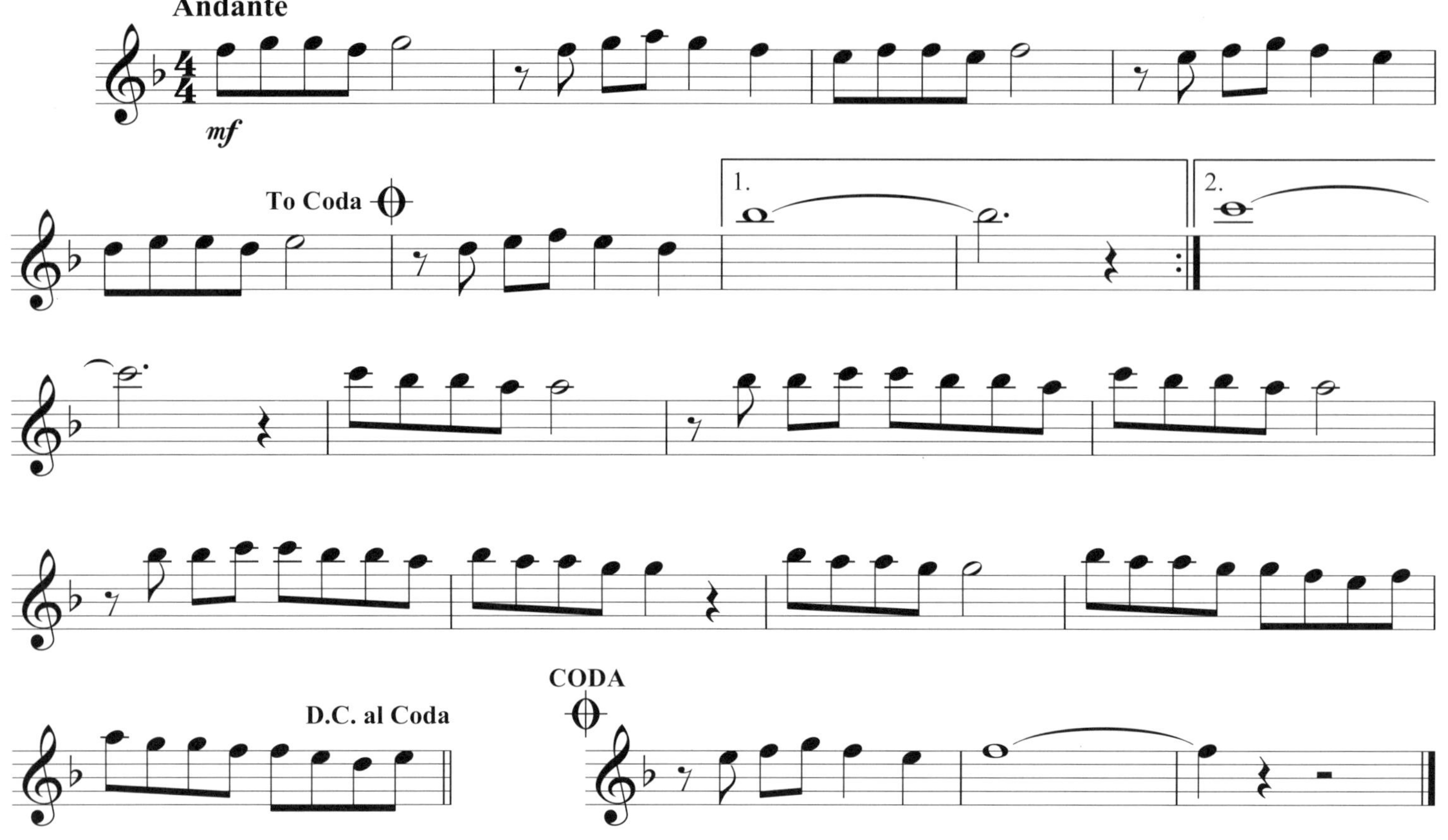

MORNING HAS BROKEN

Words by Eleanor Farjeon · Music by Cat Stevens

UNCHAINED MELODY

from the Motion Picture UNCHAINED

Lyric by Hy Zaret • Music by Alex North

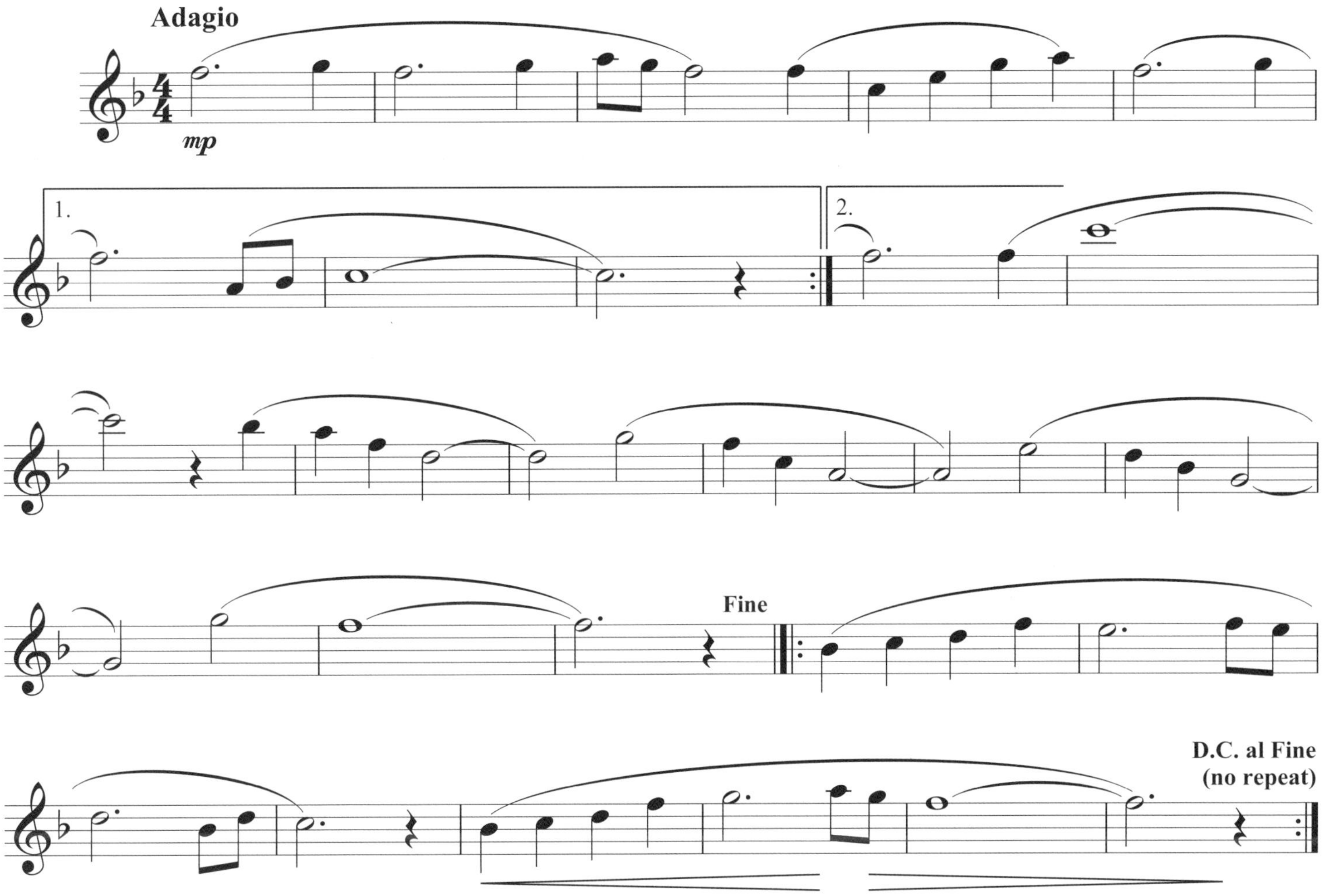
Adagio
mp
1.
2.
Fine
D.C. al Fine
(no repeat)

ROSANNA

Words and Music by David Paich

Moderate Swing
3
mf

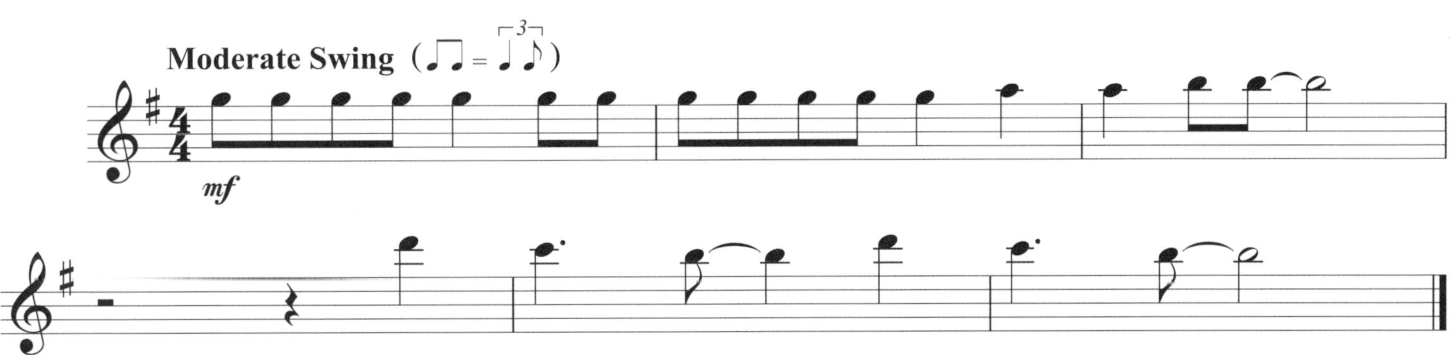

THE SURPRISE SYMPHONY

By Franz Joseph Haydn

SWING LOW, SWEET CHARIOT

Traditional Spiritual

IN THE HALL OF THE MOUNTAIN KING

from PEER GYNT

By Edvard Grieg

LOCH LOMOND

Scottish Folksong

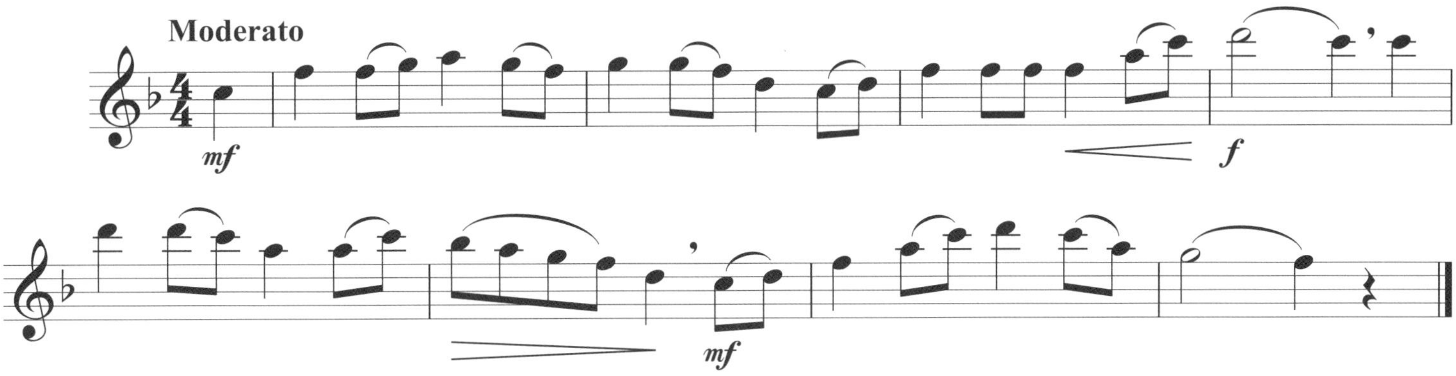

HALLELUJAH CHORUS

from MESSIAH

By George Frideric Handel

SIMPLE GIFTS

Traditional Shaker Hymn

ALL MY LOVING

Words and Music by John Lennon and Paul McCartney

MINUET

from ORPHEUS

By Christoph Willibald Gluck

LESSON 16:
High Notes

New Note: High C-Sharp/D-Flat

LIVIN' ON A PRAYER

Words and Music by Jon Bon Jovi, Desmond Child and Richie Sambora

Allegro

mf

1. 2.

f

3

ff

New Note: High D-Sharp/E-Flat

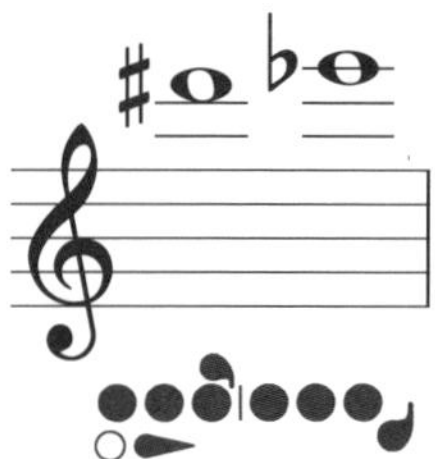

High E-flat on the flute is awesome! The fingering is easy to remember, as all fingers must be down (including both pinkies). Start good flute playing habits and resist the urge to play the E-flat fingering you already know and overblow the note. High E-flat sounds best when using the correct fingering.

Drill: E-Flat Major Scale

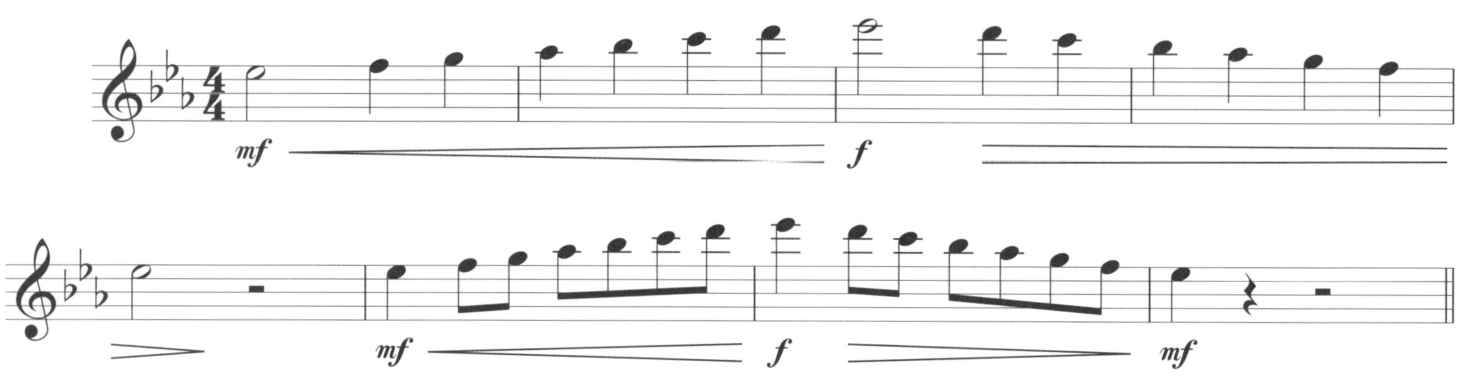

HAVANA

Words and Music by Camila Cabello, Louis Bell, Pharrell Williams, Adam Feeney, Ali Tamposi, Jeffery Lamar Williams, Brian Lee, Andrew Wotman, Brittany Hazzard and Kaan Gunesberk

FANFARE RONDEAU

from SUITE DE SYMPHONIE

By Jean-Joseph Mouret

LINUS AND LUCY

from A CHARLIE BROWN CHRISTMAS

By Vince Guaraldi

WHEN THE SAINTS GO MARCHING IN

Words by Katherine E. Purvis • Music by James M. Black

New Note: High F

Again, use the correct fingering. The middle finger on the left hand should be up. Use a higher angle of air, and practice the down-up exercise if having trouble going to or from the high F.

COUNTRY GARDENS

Traditional

New Note: High E

This can be a tough note! The high E is tricky for two reasons. One, the fingering is different. Two, it feels different than any other note. When playing the high E, you will notice that a lower note (A) can come out instead. Use plenty of air and a higher angle of air! You can do it!

BOOGIE WOOGIE BUGLE BOY

from BUCK PRIVATES

Words and Music by Don Raye and Hughie Prince

New Note: High G

SYMPHONY NO. 5

By Ludwig van Beethoven

LESSON 17:
Sixteenth Notes

A sixteenth note is worth a quarter of a beat. There are four sixteenth notes in one beat. Sixteenth notes are usually counted "1-e-&-a, 2-e-&-a, 3-e-&-a, 4-e-&-a" etc.

When two or more sixteenth notes appear, they are beamed together with two beams.

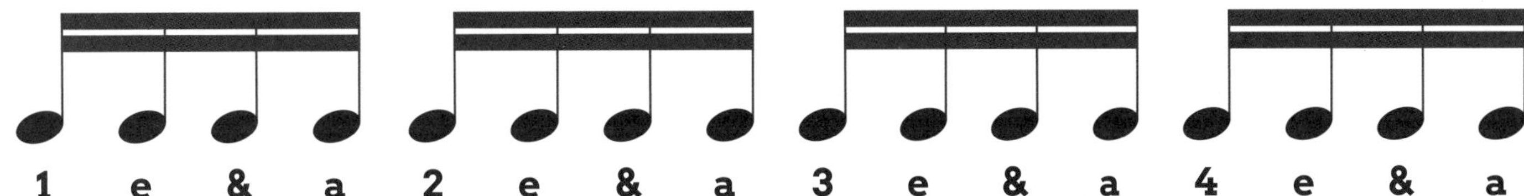

When one-sixteenth note appears, it has two flags on the stem.

TURKISH MARCH
from THE RUINS OF ATHENS
By Ludwig van Beethoven

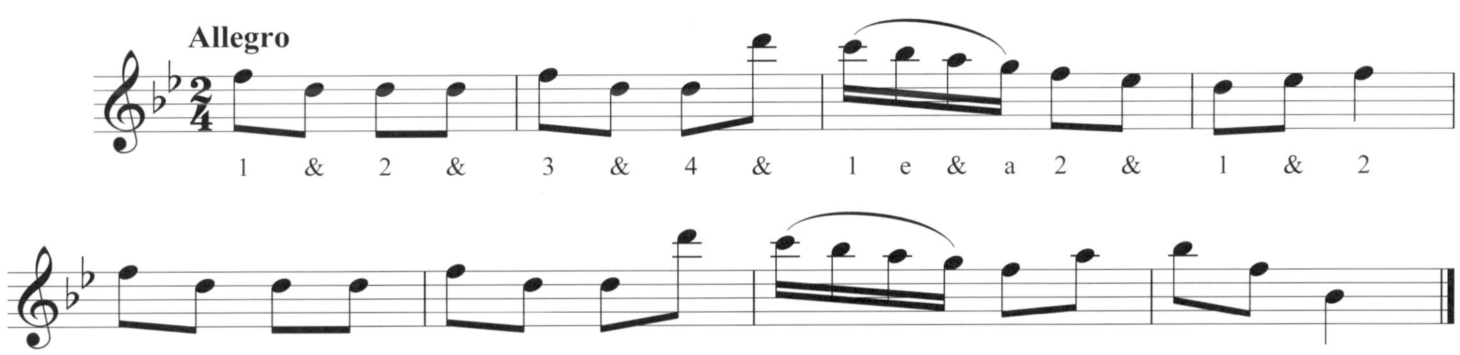

THE GOOD, THE BAD AND THE UGLY (MAIN TITLE)
from THE GOOD, THE BAD AND THE UGLY
By Ennio Morricone

THE GALWAY PIPER

Irish Folksong

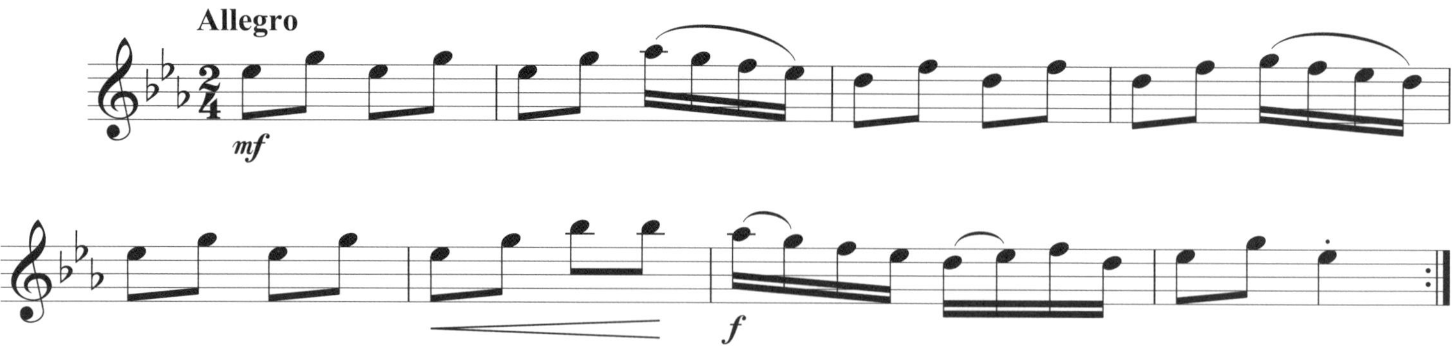

Eighth Note + Sixteenth Notes

It is common to see eighth notes and sixteenth notes beamed together when they occur within the same beat. Below you will see an eighth note followed by two sixteenth notes that are beamed together. This would be counted as "1e-&-a, 2e-&-a, 3e-&-a, 4e-&-a" etc.

THE DRUNKEN SAILOR

American Sea Chantey

UNDER PRESSURE

Words and Music by Freddie Mercury, John Deacon, Brian May, Roger Taylor and David Bowie

Dotted Eighth Note + Sixteenth Note

A rhythm many musicians encounter is the combination of a dotted eighth note followed by a sixteenth note. A dotted eighth note gets three quarters of a count, and a sixteenth note gets one quarter of a count. Together, they equal one full count. We generally count it as "1e&-a, 2e&-a, 3e&-a, 4e&-a," etc.

WEDDING MARCH

from A MIDSUMMER NIGHT'S DREAM

By Felix Mendelssohn

FUNERAL MARCH

from PIANO SONATA IN B-FLAT MINOR, OP. 35

By Fryderyk Chopin

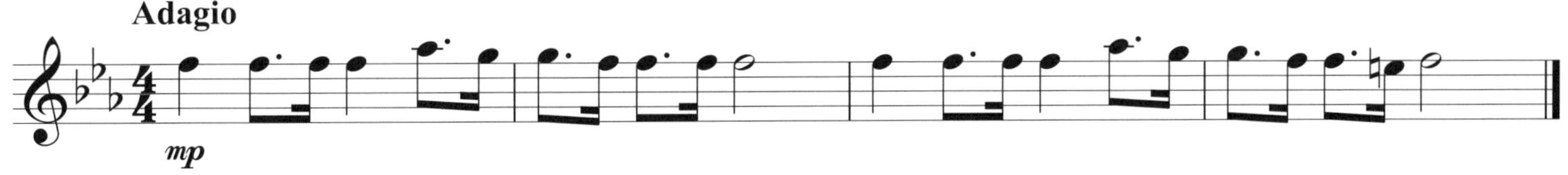

HAIL TO THE CHIEF

By James Sanderson

EYE OF THE TIGER

Theme from ROCKY III

Words and Music by Frank Sullivan and Jim Peterik

THE STAR-SPANGLED BANNER

Words by Francis Scott Key · Music by John Stafford Smith

Andante

f

Sixteenth Note + Dotted Eighth Note

The inverse of the dotted eighth plus sixteenth is the sixteenth plus dotted eighth. Instead of a "long-short-long-short" pattern, it is a "short-long-short-long" pattern. We generally count it as "1-e&a, 2-e&a, 3-e&a, 4-e&a," etc.

New Note: High F-Sharp/G-Flat

THE PINK PANTHER

from THE PINK PANTHER

By Henry Mancini

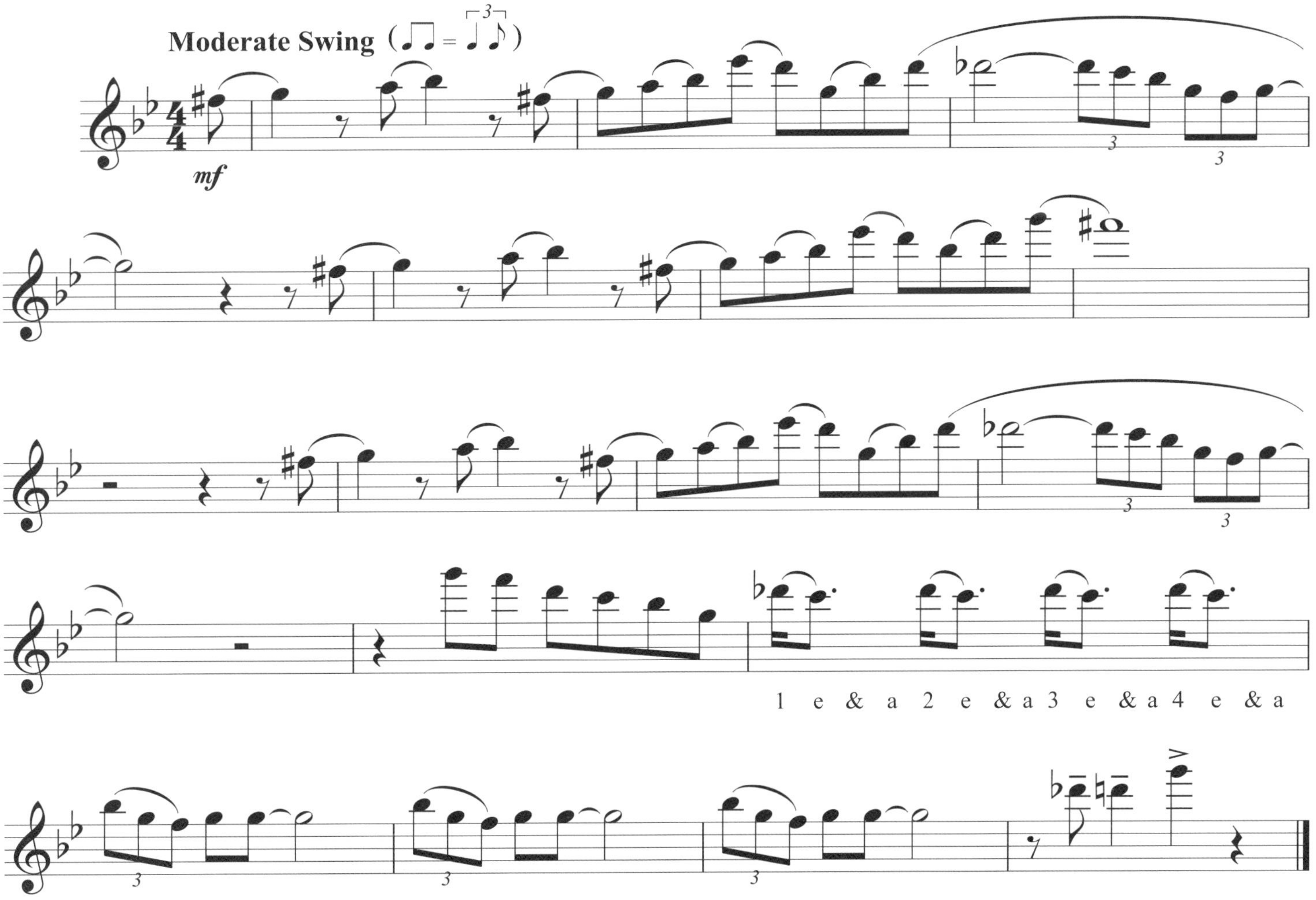

Moderate Swing

mf

1 e & a 2 e &a 3 e &a 4 e &a

LESSON 18:
Time Signatures

2/2 Time Signature

2/2 (cut time or alla breve) is a time signature in which there are two beats per measure, and the half note gets one beat. Compared to 4/4, every note value is cut in half. So, a whole note receives two beats, a half note receives one beat, and a quarter note receives half a beat. Be sure to watch the video for a more detailed explanation.

STARS AND STRIPES FOREVER

By John Philip Sousa

KARMA CHAMELEON

Words and Music by George O'Dowd, Jonathan Moss, Michael Craig, Roy Hay and Phil Pickett

IT DON'T MEAN A THING (IF IT AIN'T GOT THAT SWING)

Words and Music by Duke Ellington and Irving Mills

$\frac{6}{8}$ Time Signature

6/8 is a time signature where there are six beats per measure, and the eighth note gets one beat. When an eighth note receives one beat, a quarter note then receives two beats, a dotted quarter note receives three beats, and a dotted half note receives six beats.

6/8 time is usually played with a slight emphasis on the first and fourth beat of each measure. This divides the measure into two groups with three beats each. When practicing with a metronome, set it so each beat equals a dotted quarter.

ROW, ROW, ROW YOUR BOAT

Traditional

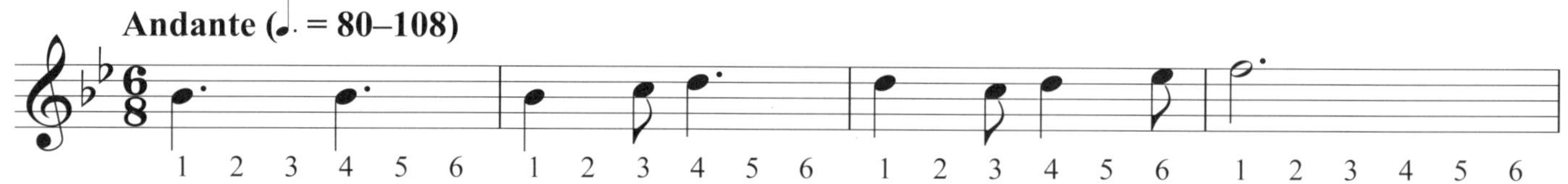

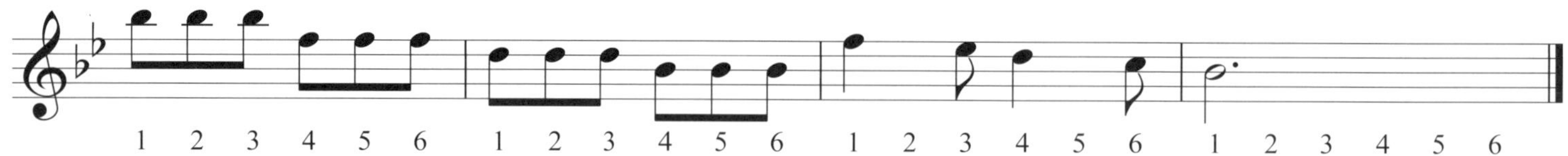

ITSY BITSY SPIDER

Traditional

FOR HE'S A JOLLY GOOD FELLOW

Traditional

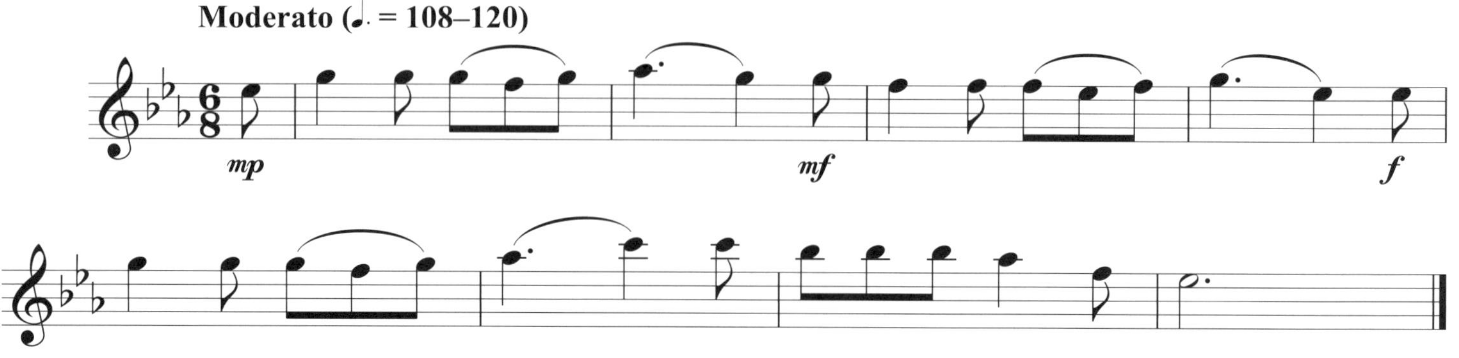

LESSON 19:
Syncopation

Syncopation occurs when an accent or emphasis is given to a note that is not on a strong beat. This type of "off-beat" feel is common in many popular and classical styles. "Pomp and Circumstance" will be used to demonstrate two common syncopations.

In 4/4 time, the primary beats are one and three. Syncopation can occur when a long note does not begin on a primary beat, as seen in the penultimate measure.

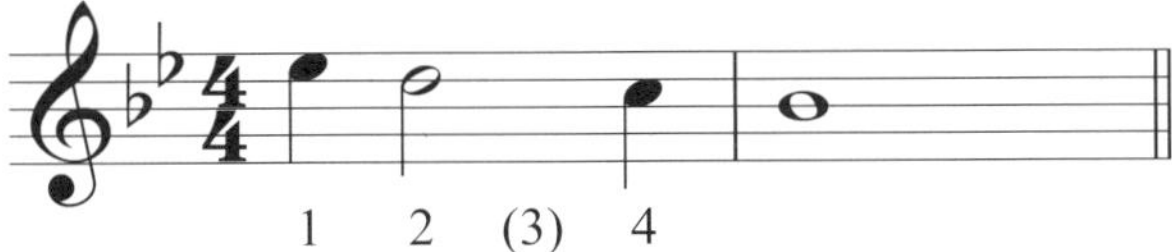

Syncopation also occurs when a longer note begins on an upbeat and is held over a downbeat. This rhythm is half the value (twice as fast) as the previous example.

POMP AND CIRCUMSTANCE

Words by Arthur Benson · Music by Edward Elgar

Before you start playing the melodies below, see if you can identify where the syncopation takes place.

YEAH!

Words and Music by James Phillips, La Marquis Jefferson, Christopher Bridges, Jonathan Smith and Sean Garrett

SCOOBY DOO, WHERE ARE YOU?

Words and Music by Ben Raleigh and David Mook

YOU'RE A GRAND OLD FLAG

Words and Music by George M. Cohan

YANKEE DOODLE DANDY

Words and Music by George M. Cohan

IMAGINE

Words and Music by John Lennon

TOOLBOX

Playing by Ear

As you progress through the book you will likely encounter some rhythms that look confusing, or you are unsure about. As you become more comfortable with various rhythms, it is oftentimes helpful to play by ear. Playing a song as you hear it in the actual recording can make deciphering rhythms easier. In the melody below, there are many ties. Feeling a tie can be awkward, so listen to the song and try to emulate what you hear. Then go back and check your work.

FIREFLIES

Words and Music by Adam Young

LESSON 20:
More Practice Songs

This chapter consists of songs in many different styles to help you put into practice all that you've learned so far. As you work through the music, remember to apply the practice tips outlined in Lesson 15.

TAKE ME OUT TO THE BALL GAME

Words by Jack Norworth · Music by Albert von Tilzer

Moderato

f

NOTRE DAME VICTORY MARCH

Lyric by John F. Shea · Music by Rev. Michael J. Shea

IF I WERE A RICH MAN

from the Musical FIDDLER ON THE ROOF

Words by Sheldon Harnick • Music by Jerry Bock

YOU ARE THE SUNSHINE OF MY LIFE

Words and Music by Stevie Wonder

DANSE BACCHANALE

from SAMSON ET DALILA (SAMSON AND DELILA)

By Camille Saint-Saens

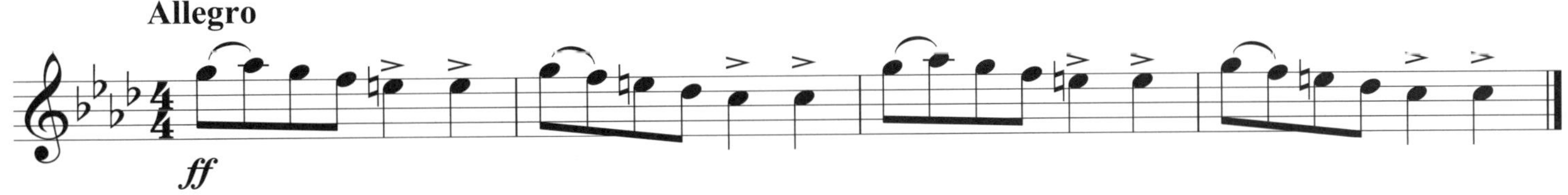

WONDERFUL WORLD

Words and Music by Sam Cooke, Herb Alpert and Lou Alder

OLD TIME ROCK & ROLL

Words and Music by George Jackson and Thomas E. Jones III

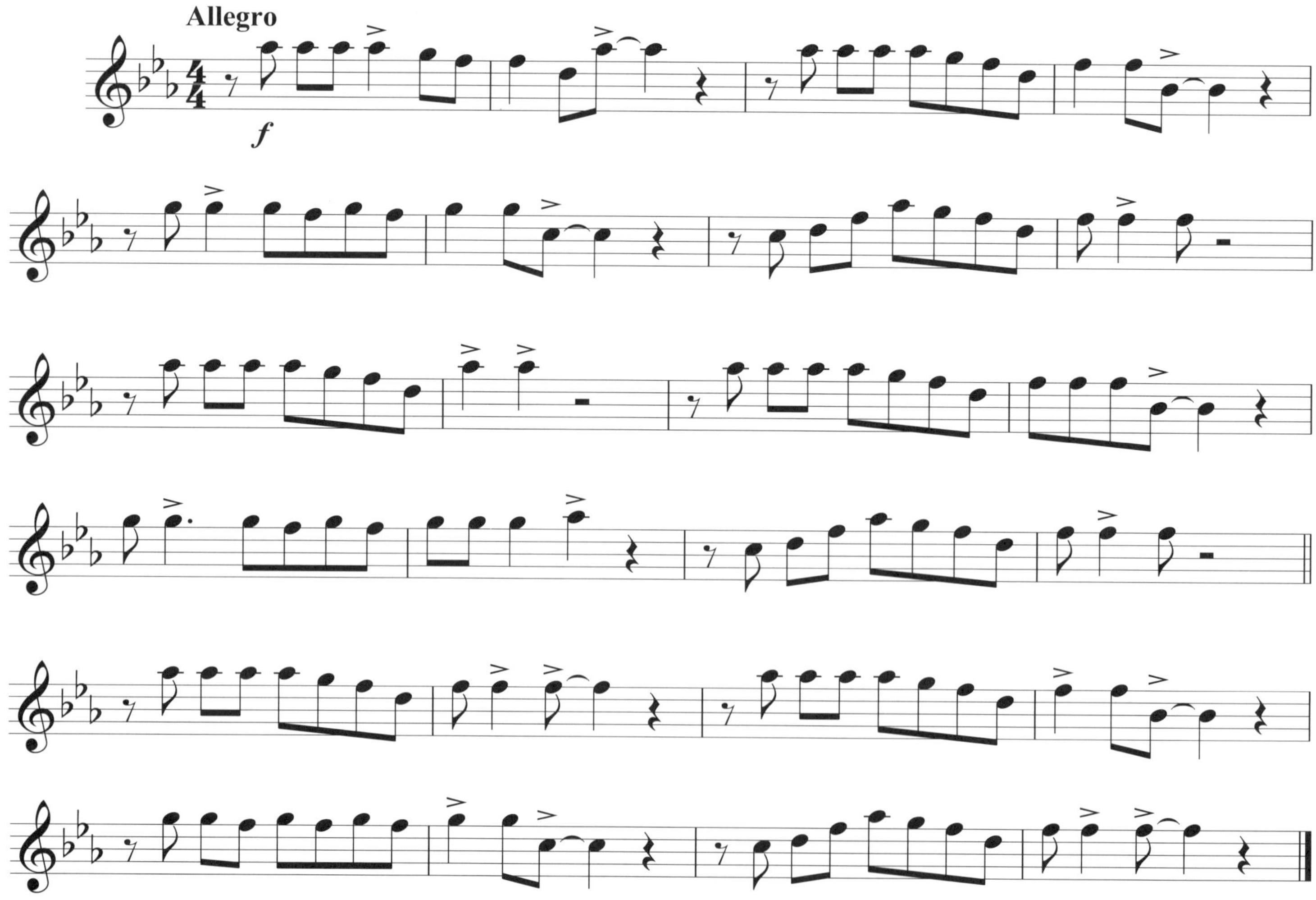

Allegro

f

HEY, SOUL SISTER

Words and Music by Pat Monahan, Espen Lind and Amund Bjorklund

POLKA DOTS AND MOONBEAMS

Words by Johnny Burke • Music by Jimmy Van Heusen

PUTTIN' ON THE RITZ

Words and Music by Irving Berlin

JUPITER

from THE PLANETS

By Gustav Holst

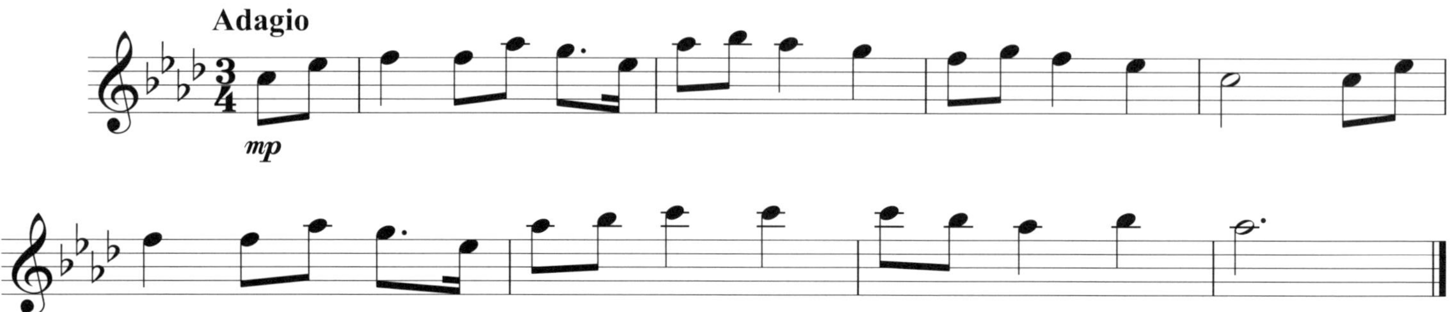

NOWHERE MAN

Words and Music by John Lennon and Paul McCartney

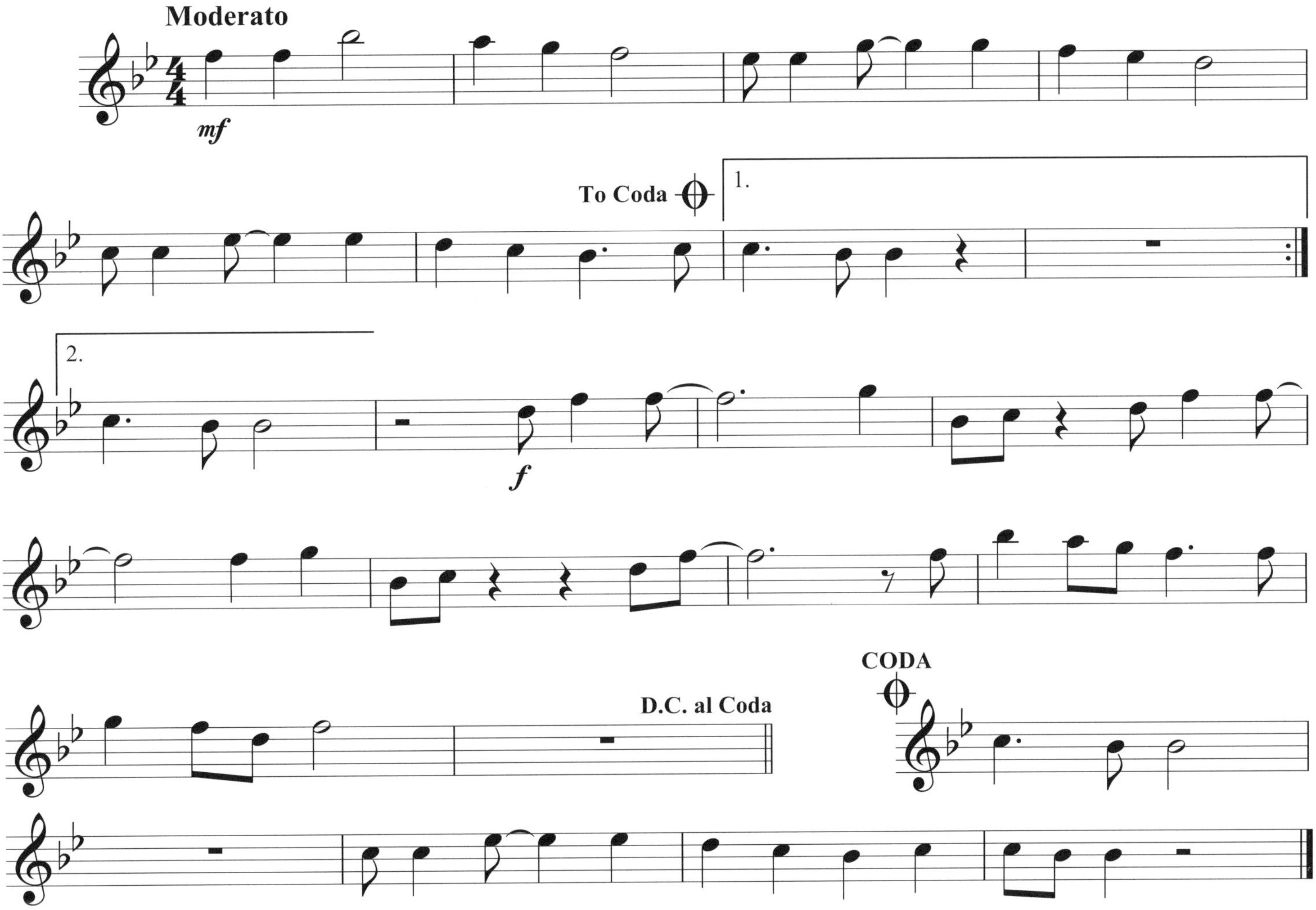

Moderato
mf
To Coda
1.
2.
f
D.C. al Coda
CODA

SEVEN NATION ARMY

Words and Music by Jack White

Allegro
3
3
3
f

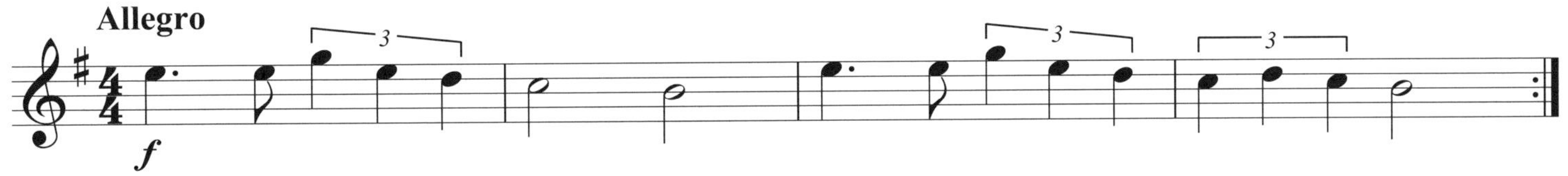

TAKE ON ME

Music by Pal Waaktaar and Magne Furuholmne
Words by Pal Waaktaar, Magne Furuholmne and Morton Harket

Vivace
f

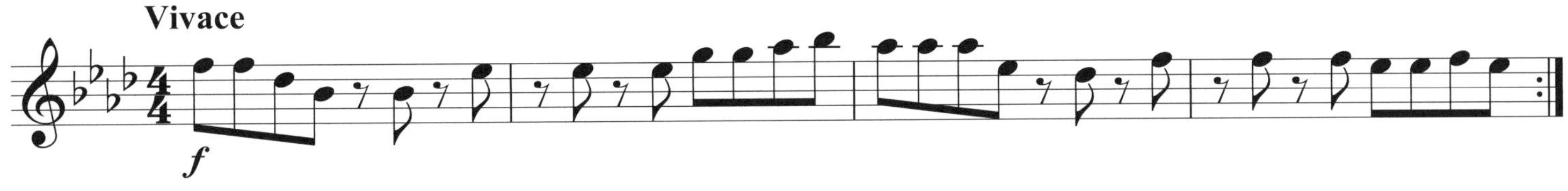

EIGHT DAYS A WEEK

Words and Music by John Lennon and Paul McCartney

THERE YOU'LL BE

from Touchstone Pictures'/Jerry Bruckheimer Films' PEARL HARBOR

Words and Music by Diane Warren

Adagio

THE AMERICAN PATROL

By F.W. Meacham

SUMMERTIME

from PORGY AND BESS®

Music and Lyrics by George Gershwin, DuBose and Dorothy Heyward and Ira Gershwin

ALL STAR

Words and Music by Greg Camp

SAKURA

Traditional Japanese Folksong

I WISH

Words and Music by Stevie Wonder

Moderato

FINAL COUNTDOWN

Words and Music by Joey Tempest

MANEATER

Words and Music by Sara Allen, Daryl Hall and John Oates

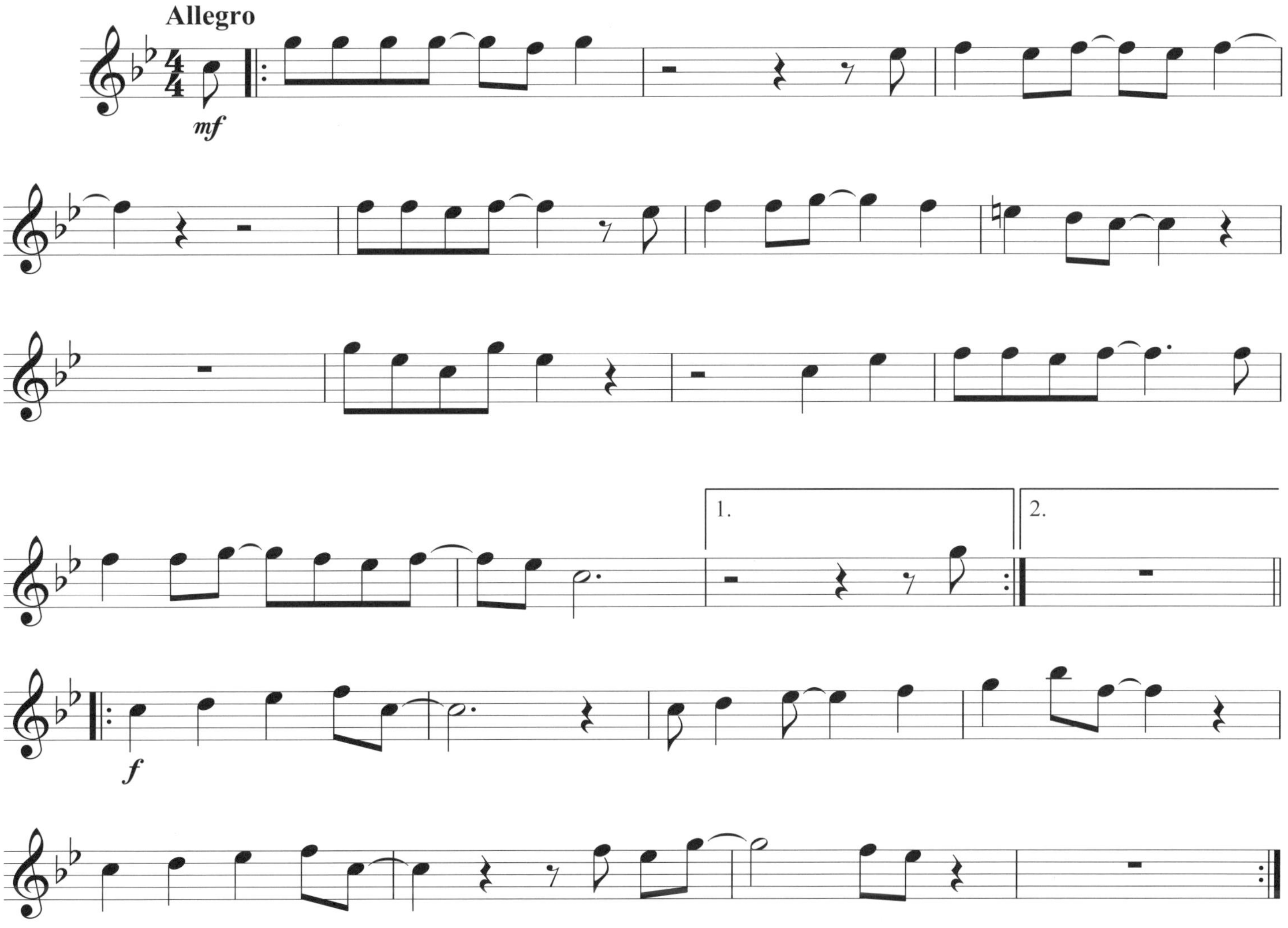
Allegro
mf
1.
2.
f

JOSHUA (FIT THE BATTLE OF JERICHO)

African American Spiritual

Allegro
mf
f
mf
f

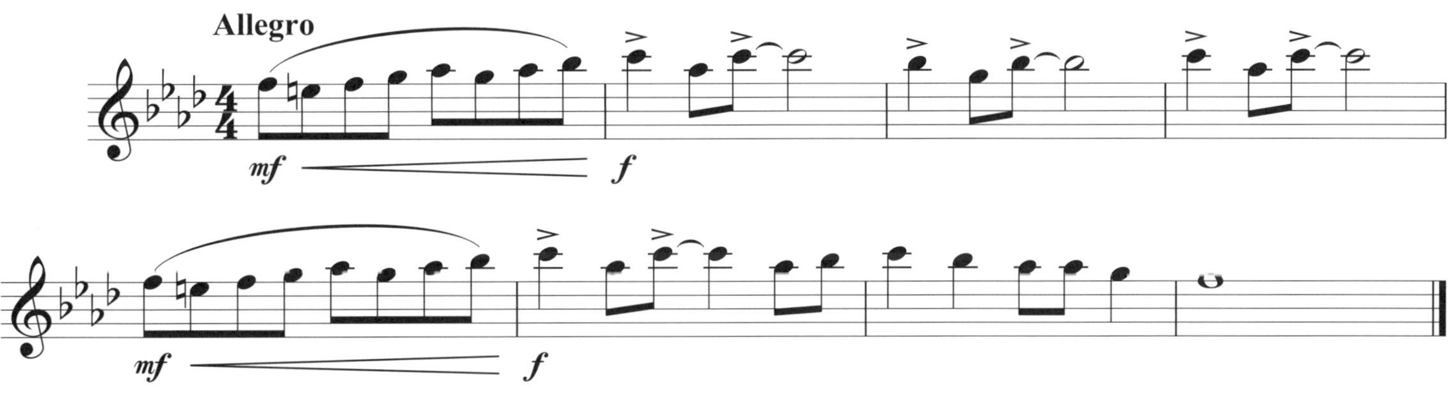

FLY ME TO THE MOON (IN OTHER WORDS)

Words and Music by Bart Howard

YESTERDAY

Words and Music by John Lennon and Paul McCartney

FIREWORK

Words and Music by Katy Perry, Mikkel Eriksen, Tor Erik Hermansen,
Esther Dean and Sandy Wilhelm

I STILL HAVEN'T FOUND WHAT I'M LOOKING FOR

Words and Music by U2

LESSON 21:
Continuing Your Journey

As you are nearing the end of this book, you have developed many of the skills necessary to perform music. It is now time to take your flute journey to the next level! Find community ensembles, chamber groups, jazz combos, rock bands or church groups to participate in. The best motivation to continue to improve is to find opportunities to showcase your skill. In this lesson, you will find advanced techniques you are likely to encounter as you continue your studies.

Vibrato

Vibrato is a technique in which a musician creates small, rapid pitch bends on a particular note. This technique allows for a characteristically beautiful, resonant tone quality. To execute this technique, take a big breath of air and exhale the air in pulses. Vibrato is best practiced on a single, long note. After some success has been achieved, add vibrato on longer notes in a melody. For this technique, be sure to watch the video. Vibrato is a wonderful skill to have as a flutist!

Drill: Vibrato Exercise #1

Repeat each measure as many times as desired. Pulse notes underneath the slur using air.

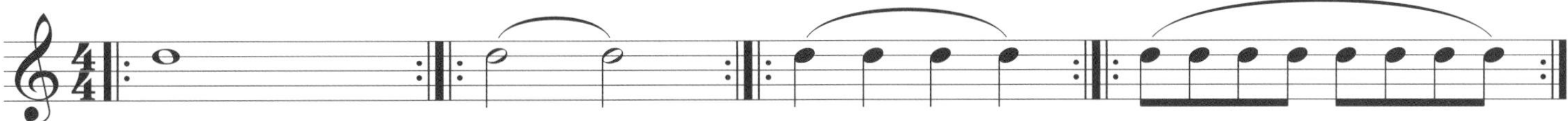

Drill: Vibrato Exercise #2

When slurring to the second note in each pair, add vibrato.

SHENANDOAH

American Folksong

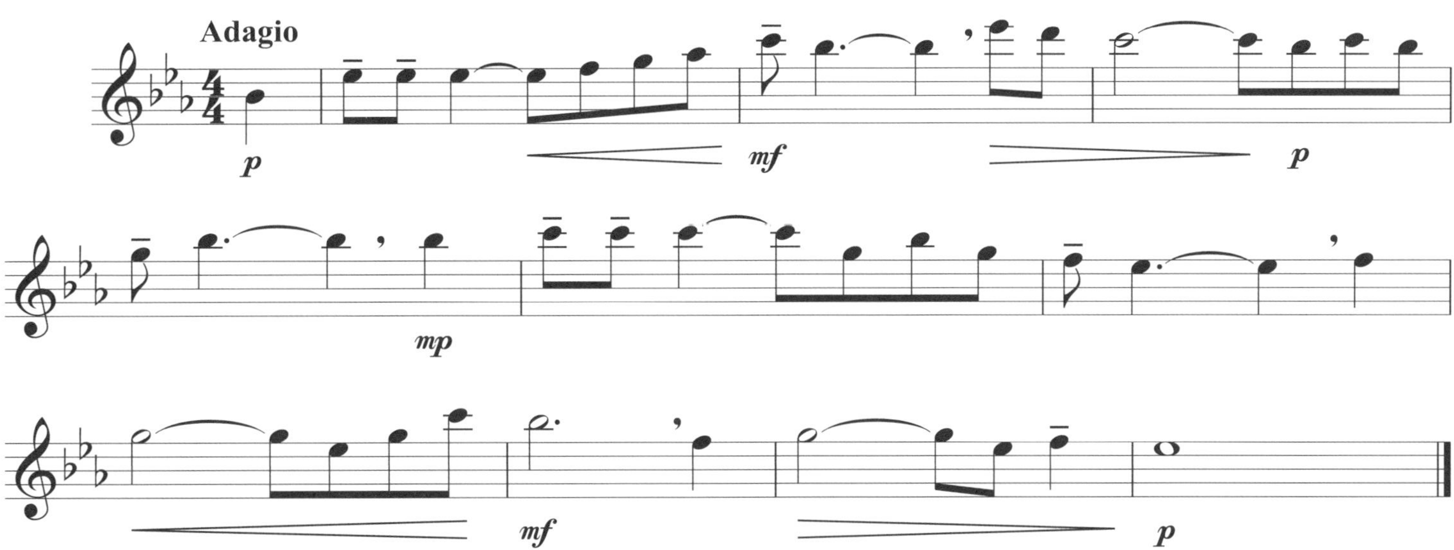

Trills *(tr)*

A *trill* is an ornamental device that allows for some interesting effects in music. It was especially popular in the Baroque and Classical periods. No doubt, you've heard trills being played and wondered how they are done. Although there are many different kinds of trills based on the type of music being played, generally, a trill is defined as the rapid alternation between two pitches. Unless specified, all trills should be executed by playing the next note in the scale above the written pitch.

For example, if the music calls for a trill on an "E," and the piece is in the key of F, then one would play as fast as possible between "E" and "F" since "F" is the next note up in the scale. If the music is in the key of G and calls for a trill on an "E," than the next note up is an "F#."

Drill: Trill Exercise

HORNPIPE

By George Frideric Handel

RANZ DES VACHES

By Gioachino Rossini

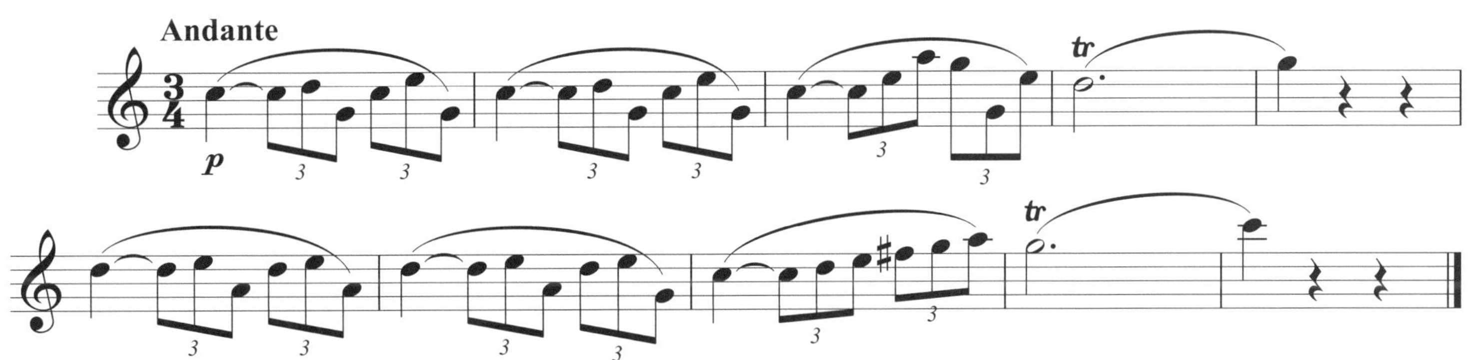

Marcato

A *marcato* is played much like a regular accent, but with a little more separation like a staccato.

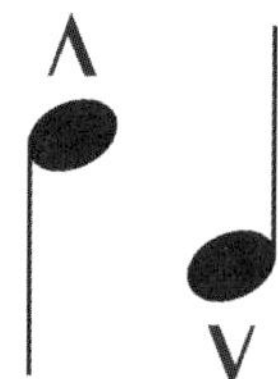

WITCHCRAFT

Music by Cy Coleman • Lyrics by Carolyn Leigh

Moderate Swing

mf

f

ff

mf

TAINTED LOVE

Words and Music by Ed Cobb

Octave Choices

Flute players have a few octaves to choose from for certain notes. If you are struggling to play some of the high notes, it is generally okay to play a note down an octave. In the melody below, there is a section that gives you a choice for which octave to play in. You can transfer this technique to other melodies in this book and beyond.

BABY ELEPHANT WALK

from the Paramount Picture HATARI!

By Henry Mancini

Dal Segno 𝄋

D.S. is the abbreviation for *Dal Segno* (the sign). When you reach the D.S. al Coda, return back to the Dal Segno and play until you reach the "To Coda" marking in the music. Then, jump to the Coda (usually near the end of the piece) and play to the end.

HEY JUDE

Words and Music by John Lennon and Paul McCartney

Time Signature Changes

A time signature (or meter) change happens when you establish a new time signature in the music. Meter changes are notated like regular time signatures, however, unlike the initial time signature established at the beginning of a piece, meter changes can happen anywhere in the song.

Counting can be especially tricky during time signature changes, so make sure you take the time to feel the number of beats correctly.

ALL YOU NEED IS LOVE

Words and Music by John Lennon and Paul McCartney

Key Signature Changes

A key signature change happens when you change keys in a piece of music. Key changes are notated like regular key signatures, however, unlike the initial key signature established at the beginning of a piece, key changes can happen anywhere in the song.

Remembering proper sharps and flats can be especially tricky during key signature changes. Make sure you take time to identify where the key change(s) take place and mark your music accordingly.

TIME IN A BOTTLE

Words and Music by Jim Croce

VOCABULARY TERMS

A tempo: return to the original tempo

Accelerando: gradually speed up

Accent: an articulation, attack note by playing stronger

Accidental: sharp, flat, or natural that appears in a measure

Adagio: slow tempo, ♩ = 60-80

Allegro: fast tempo, ♩ = 120-156

Andante: slower "walking" tempo, ♩ = 80-108

Aperture: the opening that air leaves your mouth and enters the tone hole on the head joint

Articulation: style in which you attack, or tongue each note

Bar line: divides the music staff into measures

Breath mark: indicates where to breathe

Coda: the conclusion

Common time: another way to notate 4/4

Crescendo: gradually get louder

Cut time: value of each beat from 4/4 is cut in half, also notated as 2/2

Da Capo (D.C.): from the beginning

Dal Segno (D.S.): from the sign

Decrescendo: gradually get softer

Dot: adds half of the value of the note

Double bar: indicates a new section within the music

Dynamics: indicate how loud or soft to play

Embouchure: position of mouth on the tone hole

Enharmonic: two notes with the same pitch but written with different note names

Fermata: hold for a longer, unspecified time

Fine: the end

Flat: lowers note a half-step

Forte: loud

Fortissimo: very loud

Forward repeat: repeat sign at the beginning of a measure

Interval: distance between notes

Intonation: pitch accuracy

Key signature: indicates whether to play the notes sharp, flat, or natural

Largo: very slow tempo, ♩ = 40-60

Ledger lines: lines that extend the music staff

Marcato: an articulation, with a strong attack and separation between notes

Measure: space between two bar lines

Meter: a regular recurring pattern of beats; time signature

Metronome: device used to keep a steady tempo

Mezzo forte: medium loud

Mezzo piano: medium soft

Moderato: medium tempo, ♩ = 108-120

Natural: cancels sharps or flats to return note back to its normal state

Octave: interval that is eight notes apart, both notes have the same name

Offbeat: a beat that does not fall on a strong beat

Phrase: musical sentence, or complete idea

Piano: soft

Pickup note: note or group of notes that occur before the first full measure

Presto: very, very fast, ♩ = 176 and up

Rallentando: gradually slow down

Ritardando: gradually slow down

Sharp: raises note a half-step

Slur: an articulation, connects two or more notes of any pitch

Staccato: an articulation, light and separated

Staff: lines and spaces where music is written

Subdivision: breaking the beat into smaller, even pieces

Swing: musical style where eighth notes are not even in length

Syncopation: rhythmic change where emphaisis shifts to the offbeat

Tempo: speed of the music

Tenuto: an articulation, note is held full value

Tie: connects two or more notes of the same pitch together

Time signature: indicates number of beats in a measure as well which type of note receives one beat

Tone: sound produced with the instrument

Treble clef: also known as G clef; the clef used for flute players

Trill: rapidly moving back and forth between two notes that are next to each other

Triplet: three notes of equal length grouped together

Vibrato: rapid bending of a pitch

Vivace: very fast, ♩ = 156-176

FINGERING CHART

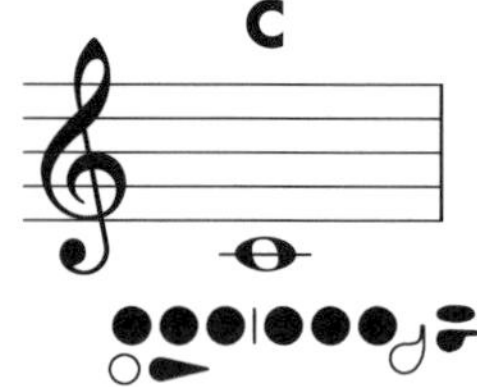

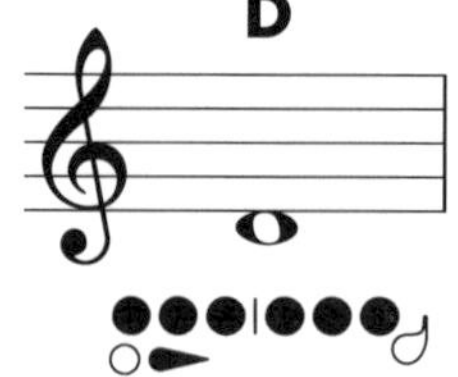

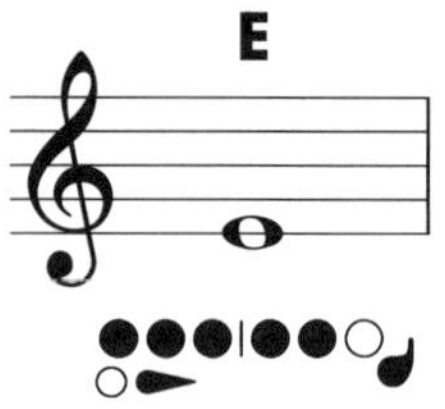

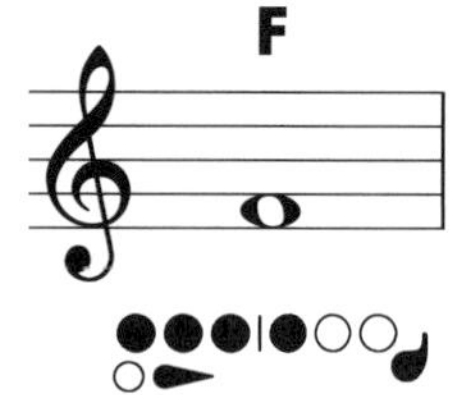

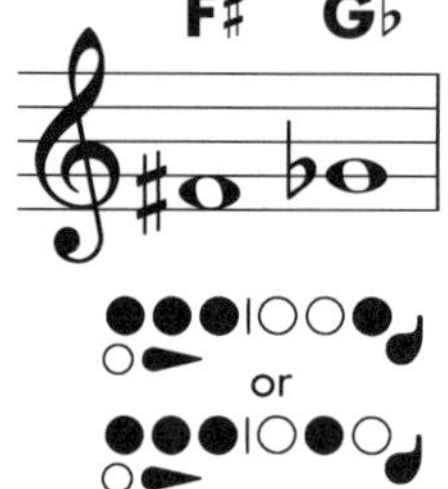

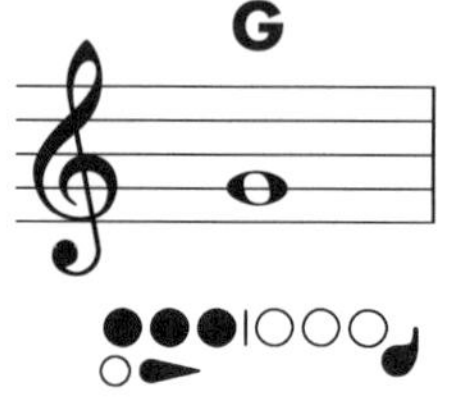

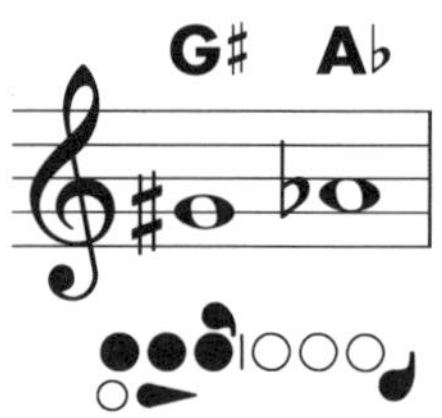

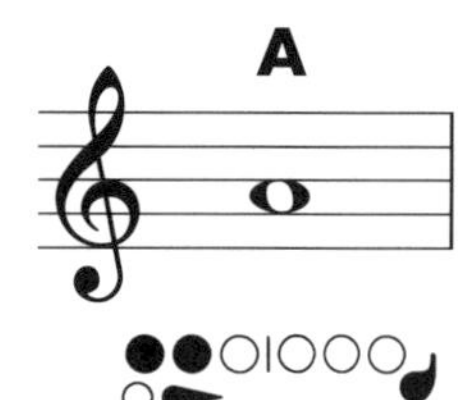

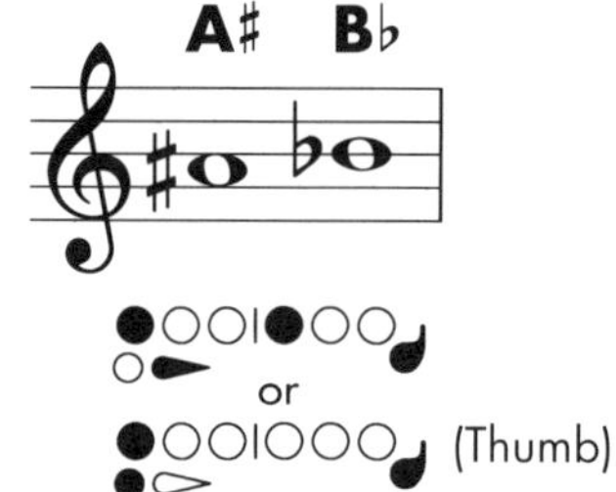

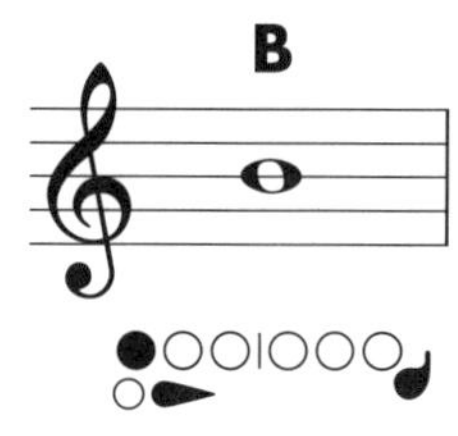

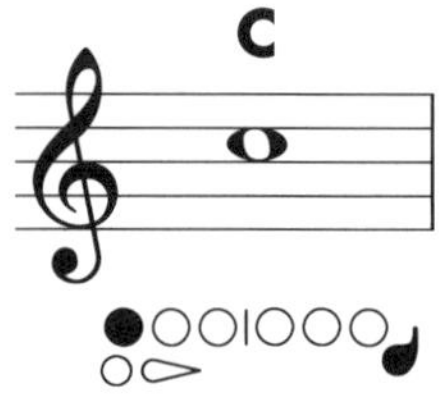

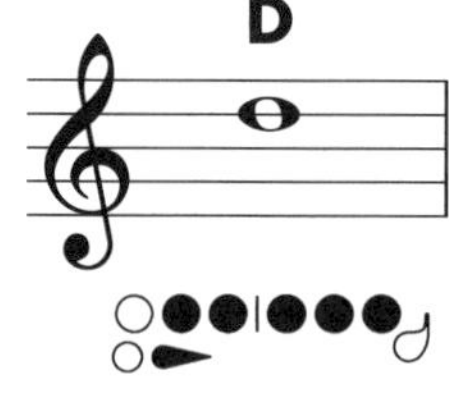

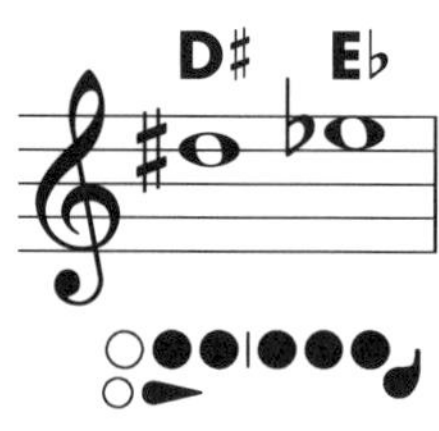

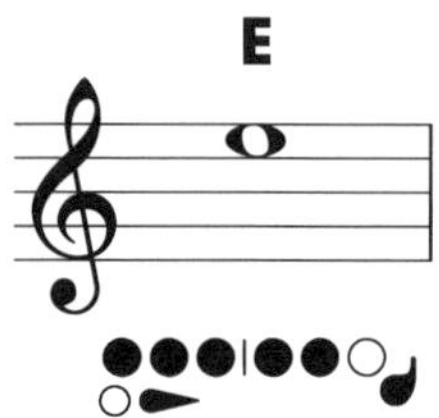

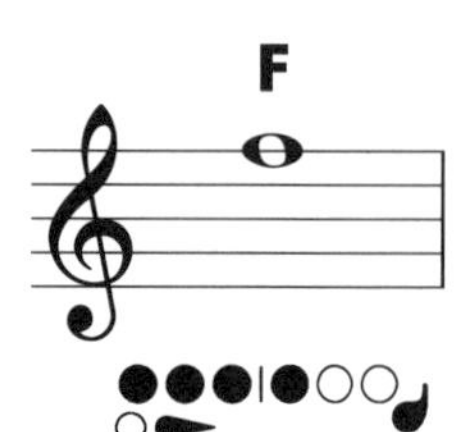

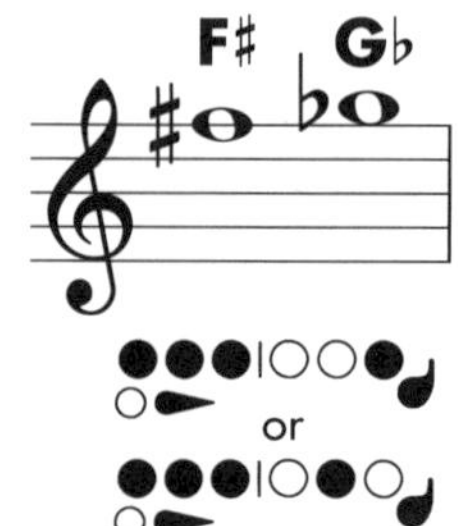

G♯ A♭
A
A♯ B♭
or
(Thumb)
B
C
C♯ D♭
D
D♯ E♭
E
F
F♯ G♭
or
G
G♯ A♭
or
A
A♯ B♭
or
B
C

TRILL CHART

E → F
tr
A → B♭
tr
or
D → E
tr

E → F♯
tr

F♯ → G
tr

A♭ → B♭
tr

A → B
tr

B♭ → C
tr
or

B → C♯
tr

C → D♭
tr
C♯ → D

D♭ → E♭
tr

D → E♭
tr

E♭ → F
tr

G → A♭
tr

B♭ → C
tr
or

B → C
tr

C → D
tr

C♯ → D
tr

D♭ → E♭
tr

D → E♭
tr
or

D → E
tr

E♭ → F
tr
or

E → F
tr

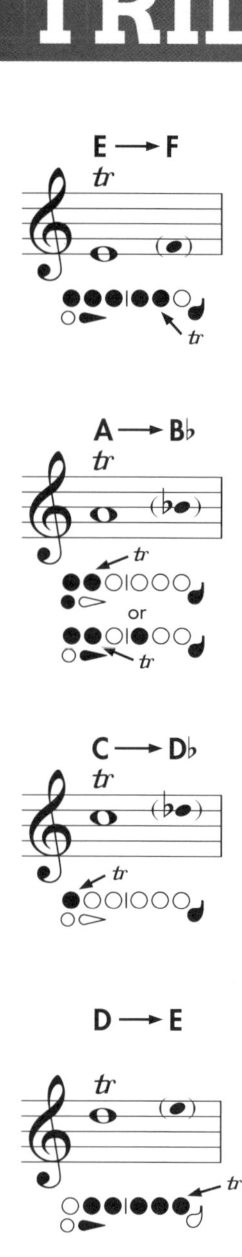

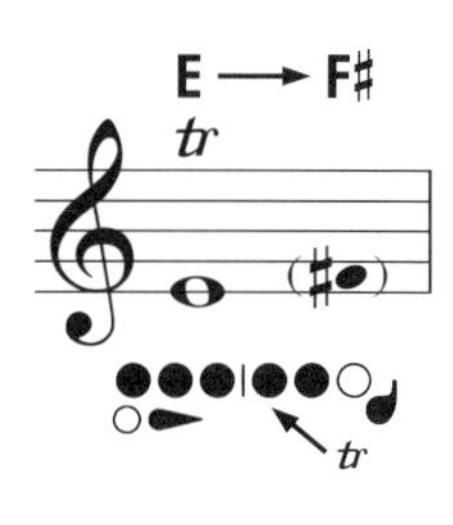

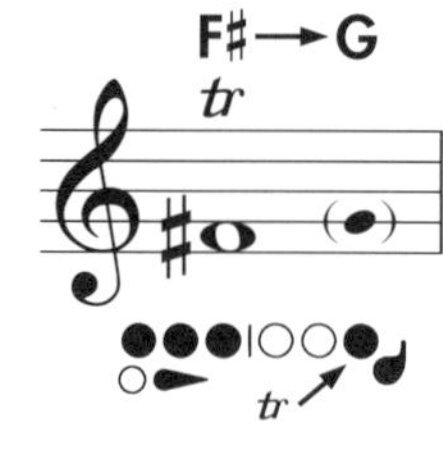

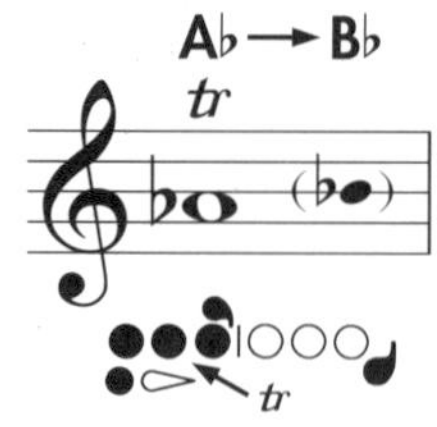

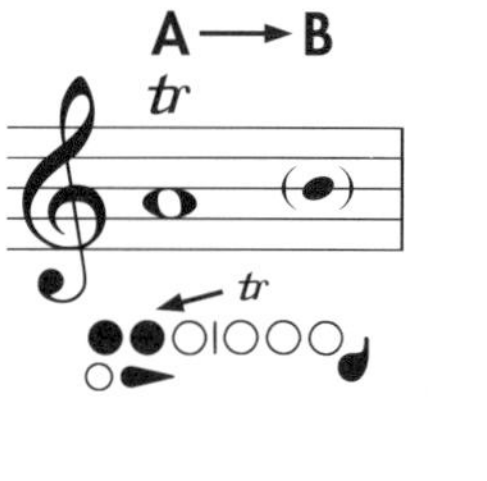

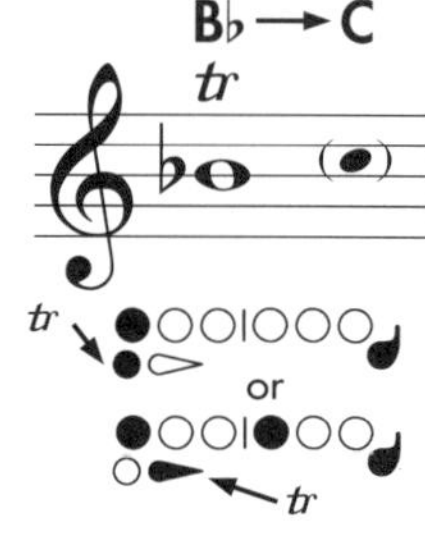

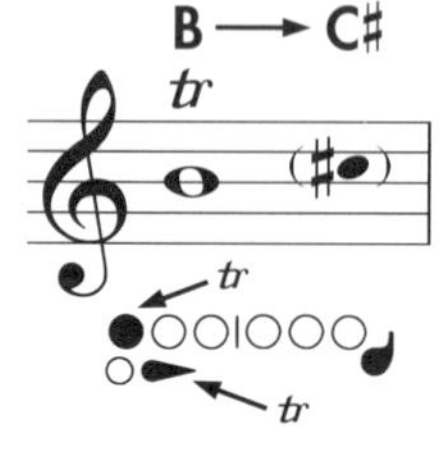

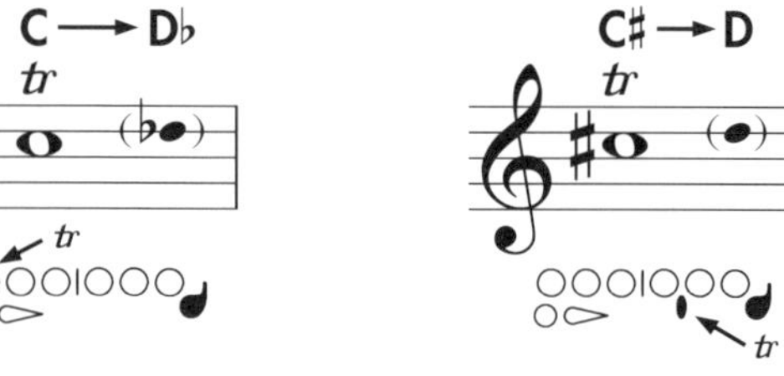

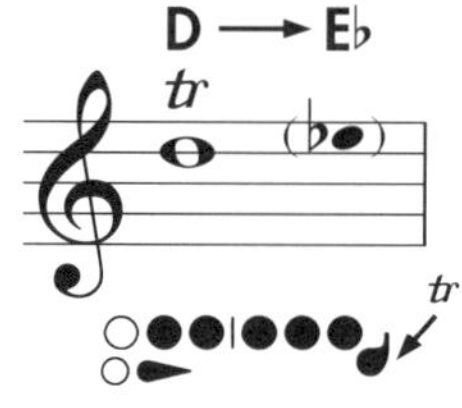

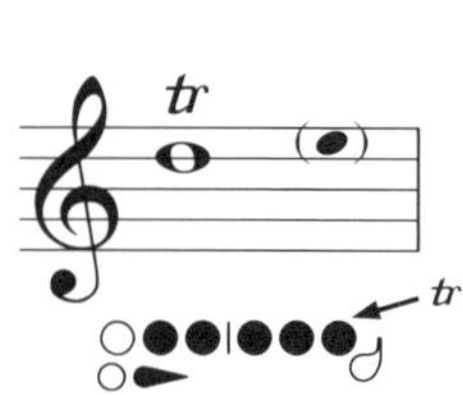

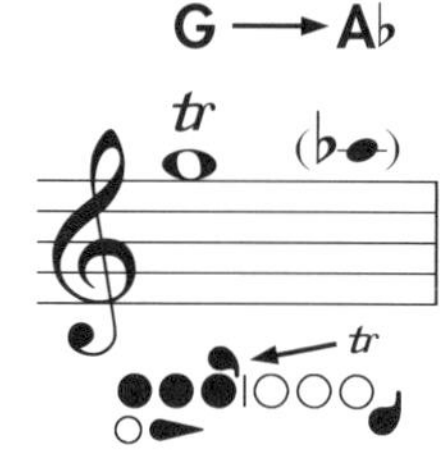

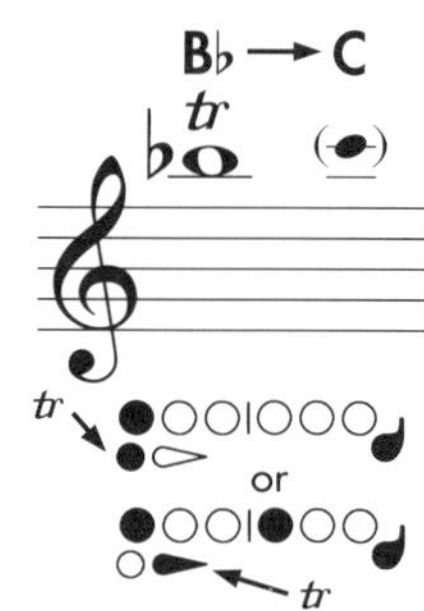

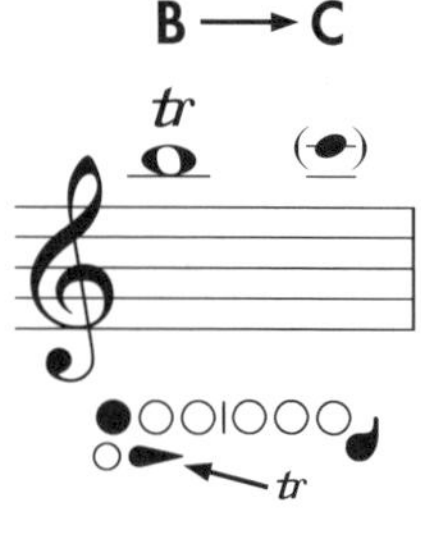

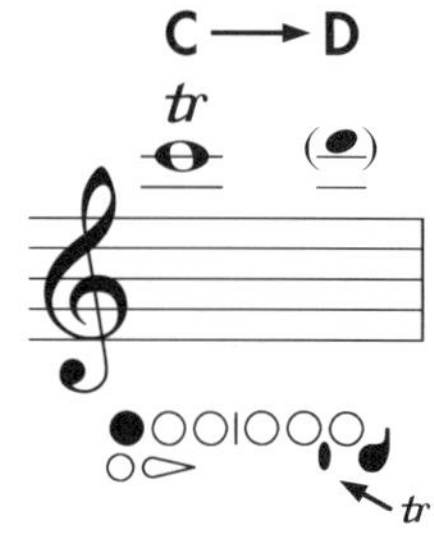

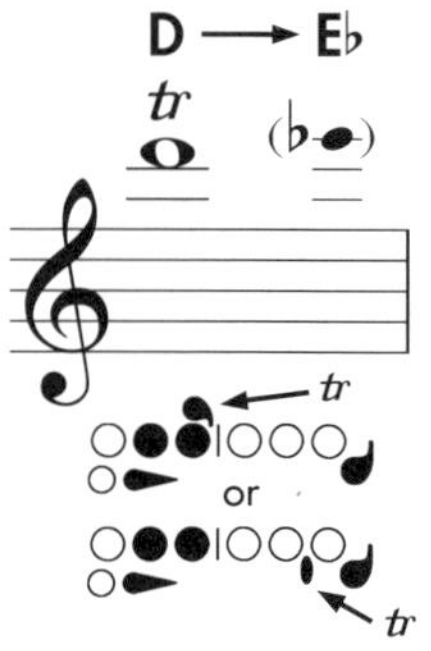

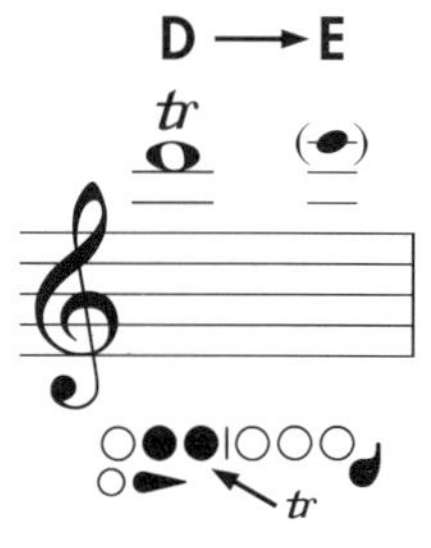

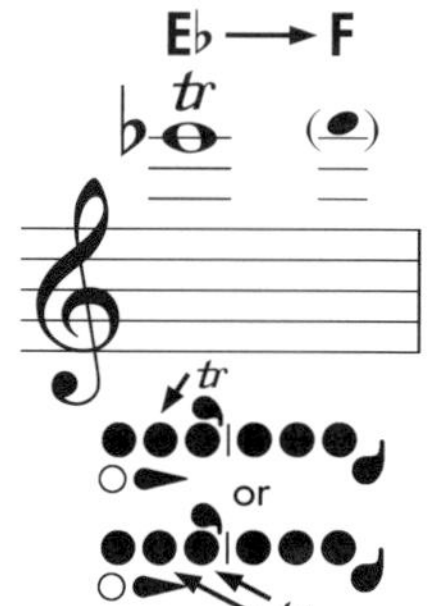

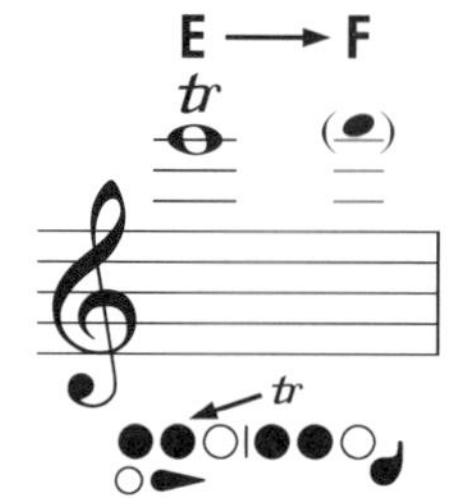